FIRST 50 SONGS
YOU SHOULD PLAY ON SOLO UKULELE

ISBN 978-1-5400-4609-3

Visit Hal Leonard Online at
www.halleonard.com

Contact Us:
Hal Leonard
7777 West Bluemound Road
Milwaukee, WI 53213
Email: info@halleonard.com

In Europe, contact:
Hal Leonard Europe Limited
42 Wigmore Street
Marylebone, London, W1U 2RN
Email: info@halleonardeurope.com

In Australia, contact:
Hal Leonard Australia Pty. Ltd.
4 Lentara Court
Cheltenham, Victoria, 3192 Australia
Email: info@halleonard.com.au

Africa

Words and Music by David Paich and Jeff Porcaro

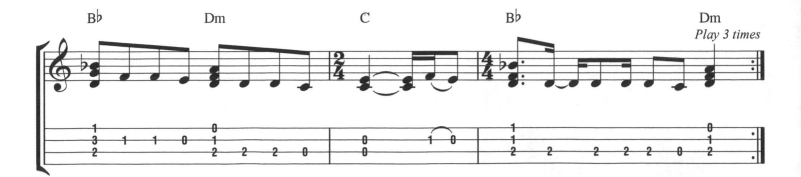

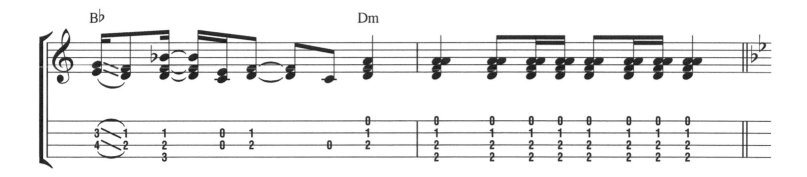

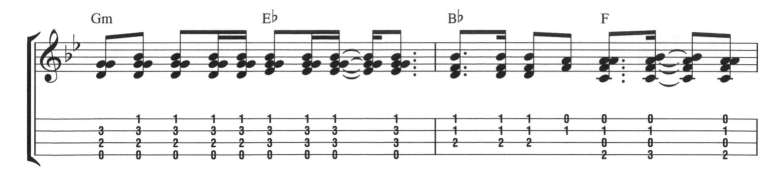

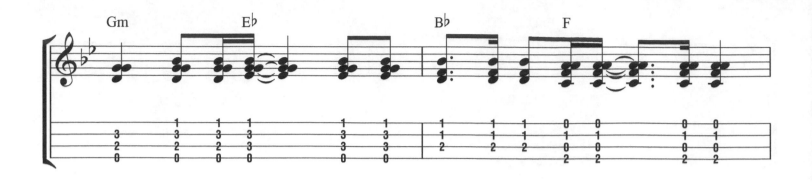

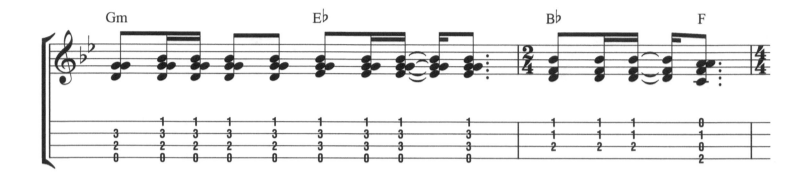

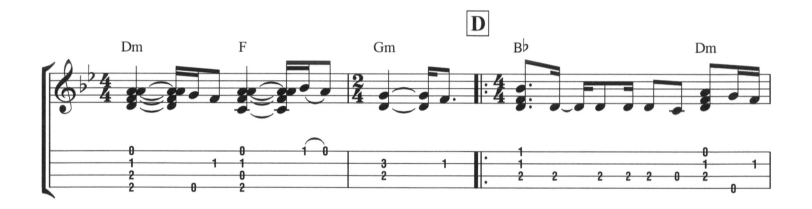

All of Me

Words and Music by John Stephens and Toby Gad

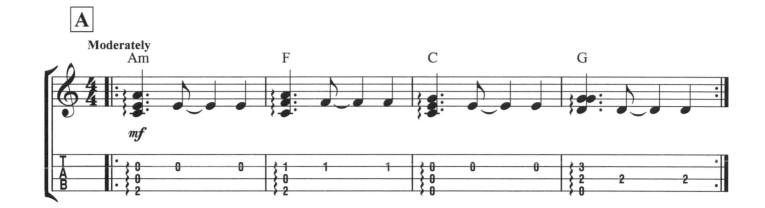

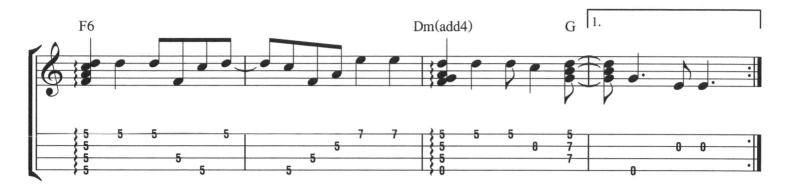

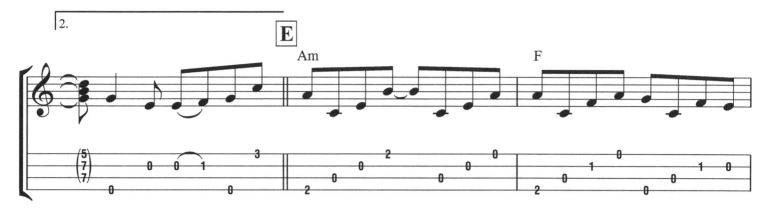

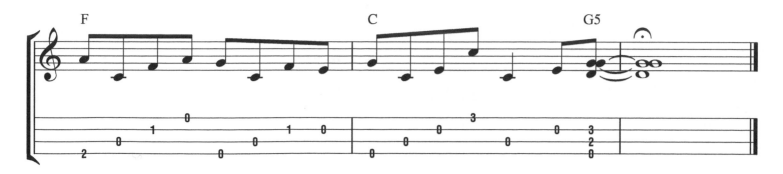

All I Ask of You

from THE PHANTOM OF THE OPERA

Music by Andrew Lloyd Webber
Lyrics by Charles Hart
Additional Lyrics by Richard Stilgoe

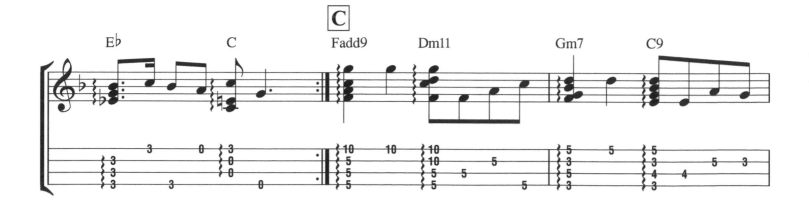

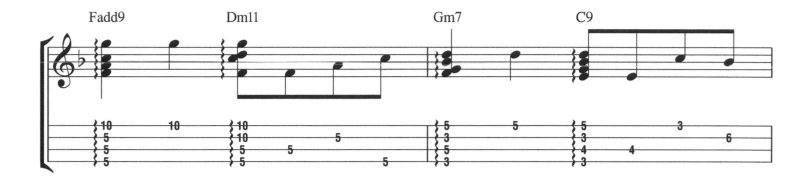

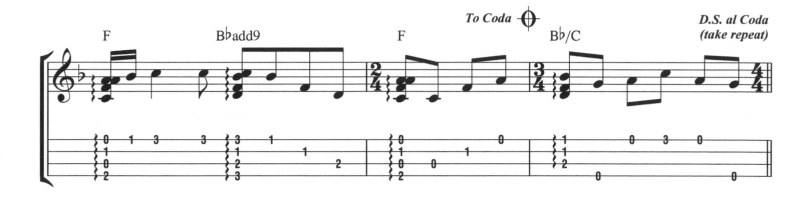

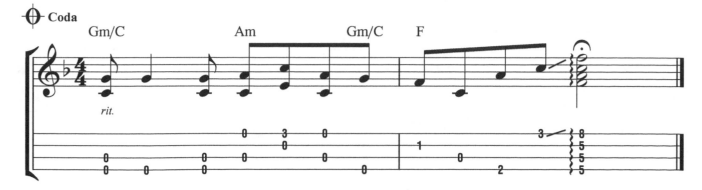

Amazing Grace

Words by John Newton
From A Collection of Sacred Ballads
Traditional American Melody
From Carrell and Clayton's Virginia Harmony

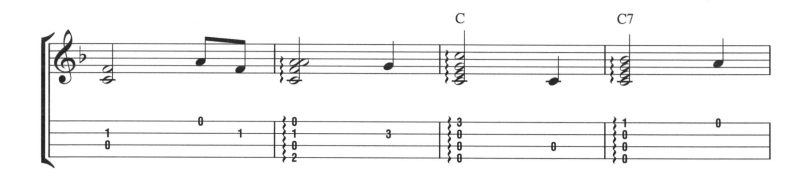

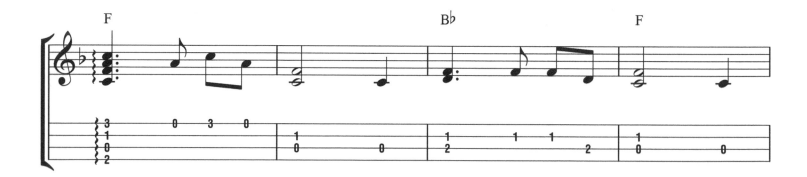

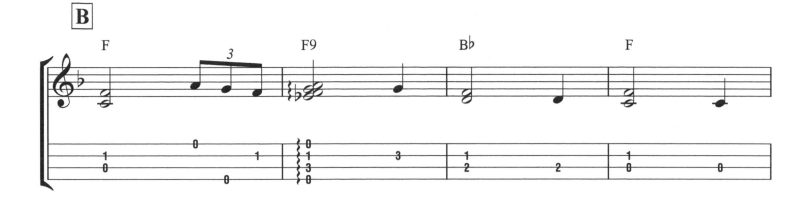

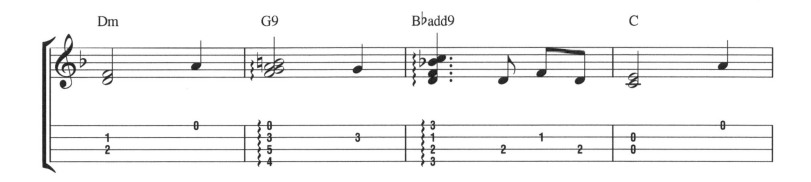

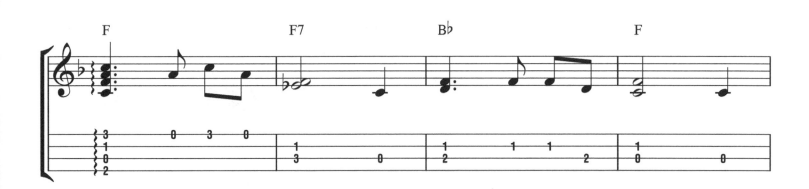

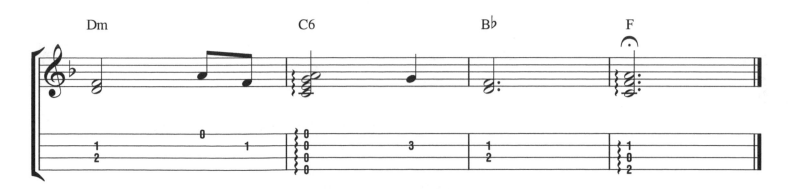

Autumn Leaves

English lyric by Johnny Mercer
French lyric by Jacques Prevert
Music by Joseph Kosma

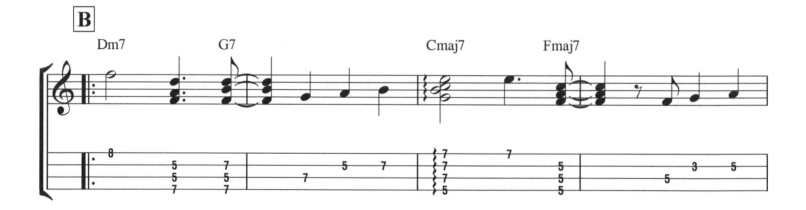

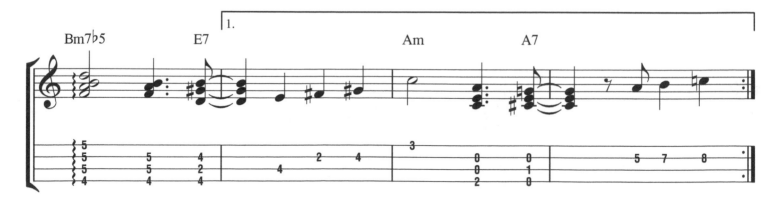

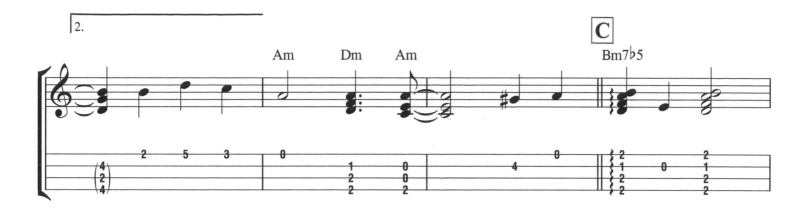

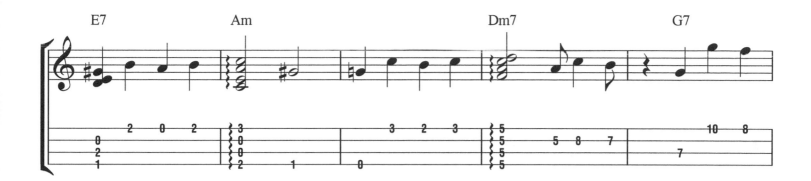

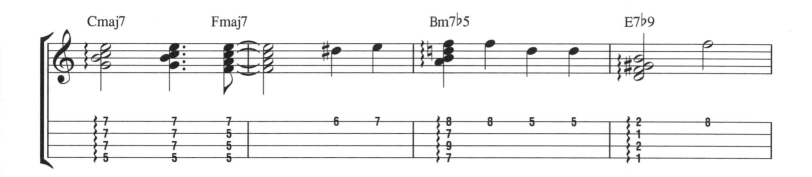

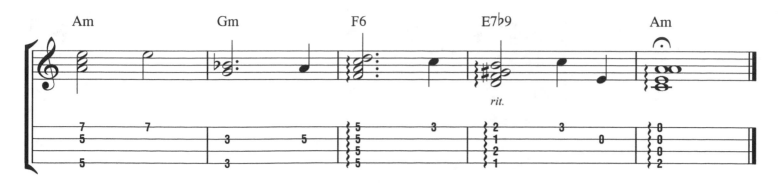

Blackbird

Words and Music by John Lennon and Paul McCartney

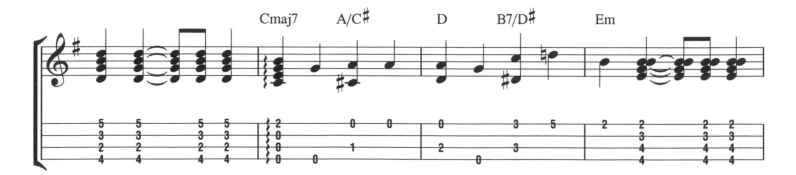

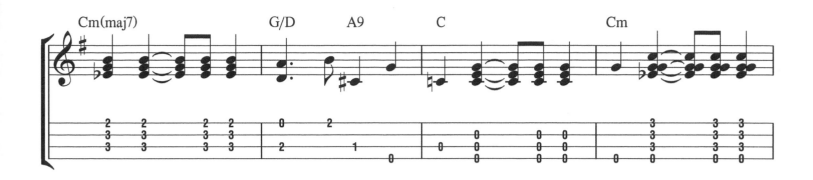

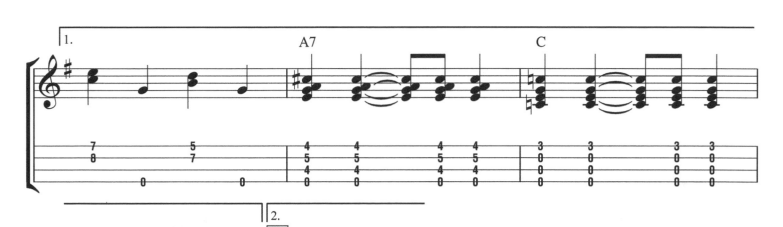

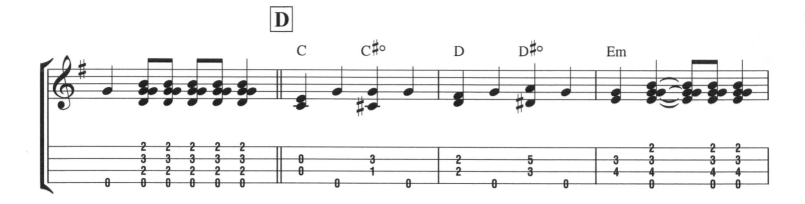

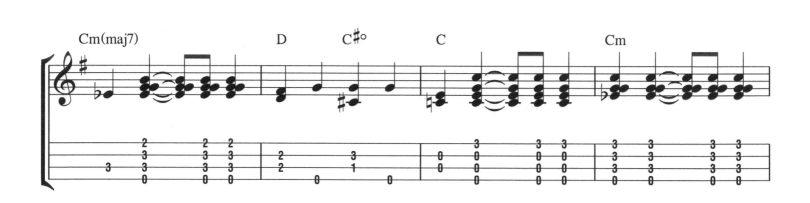

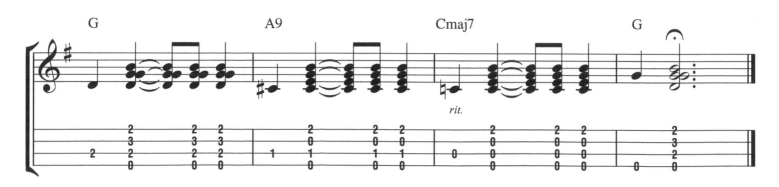

Blowin' in the Wind

Words and Music by Bob Dylan

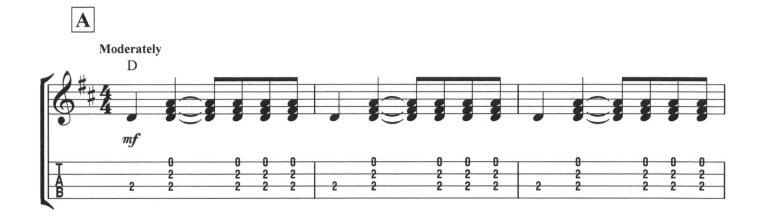

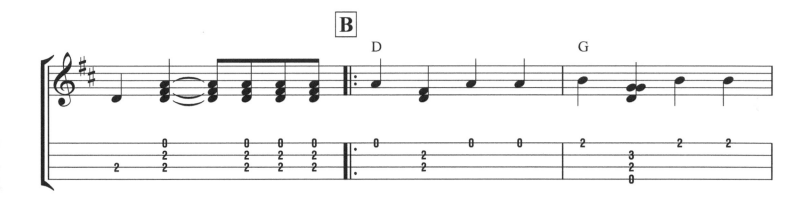

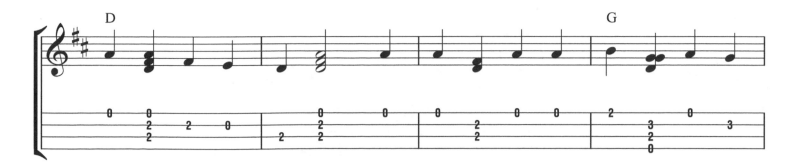

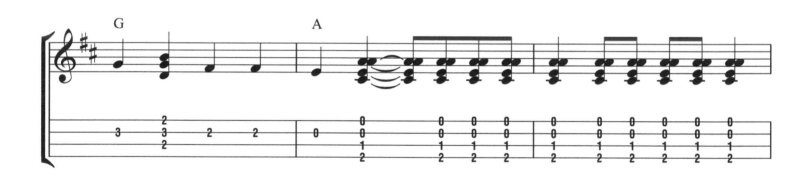

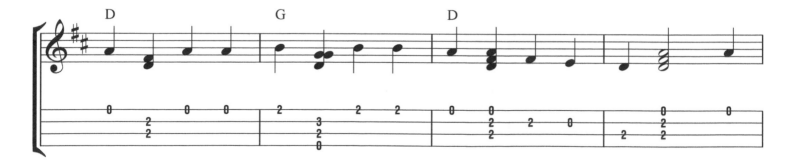

Blue Skies

from BETSY

Words and Music by Irving Berlin

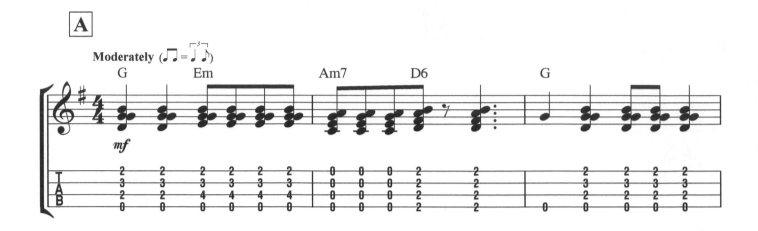

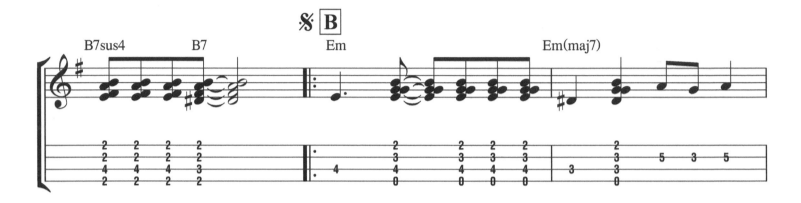

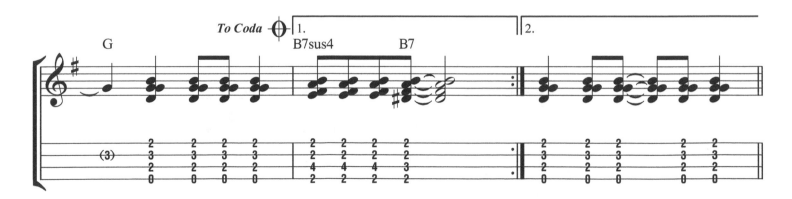

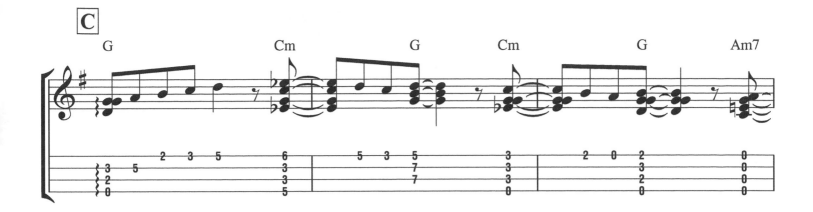

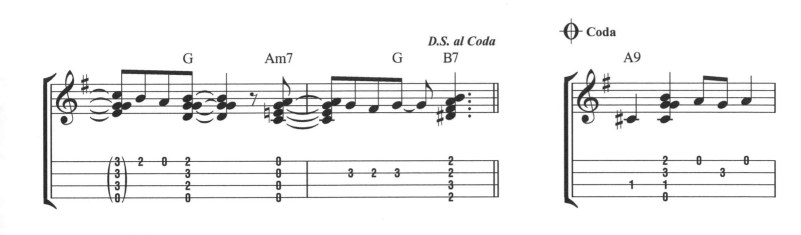

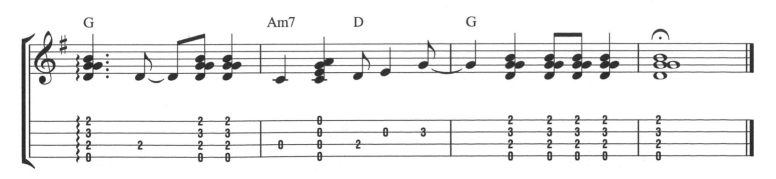

Body and Soul

from THREE'S A CROWD

Words by Edward Heyman, Robert Sour and Frank Eyton
Music by John Green

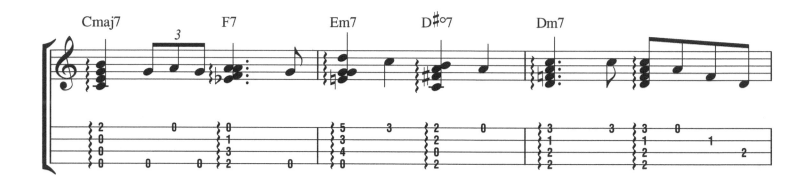

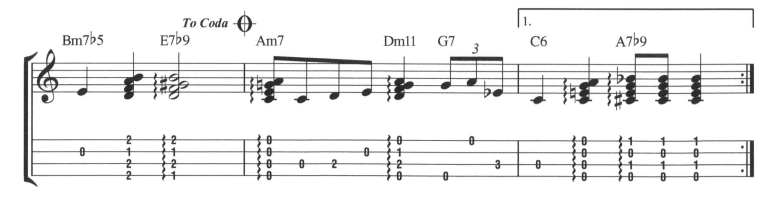

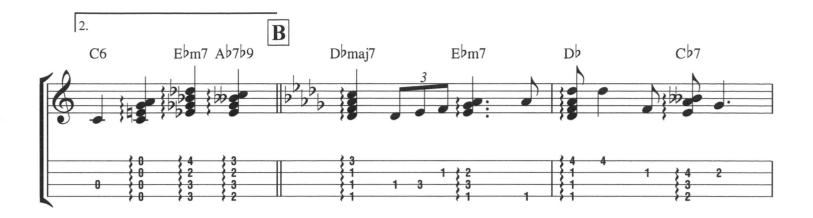

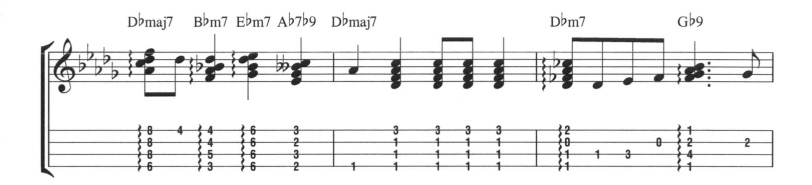

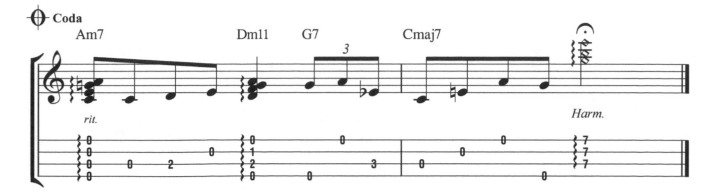

The Boxer

Words and Music by Paul Simon

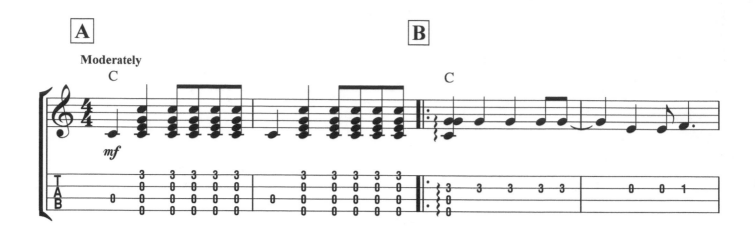

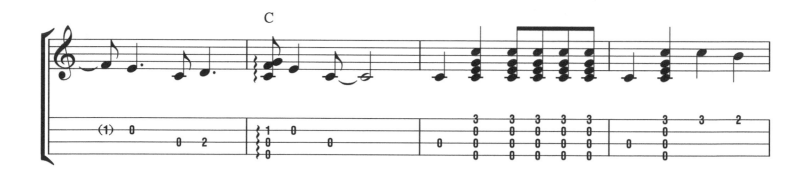

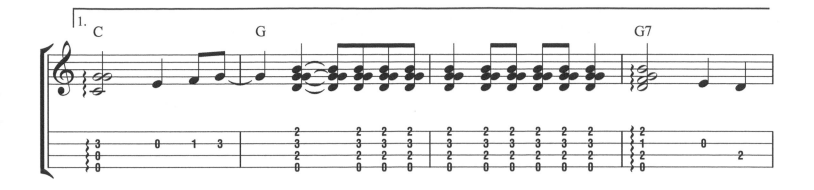

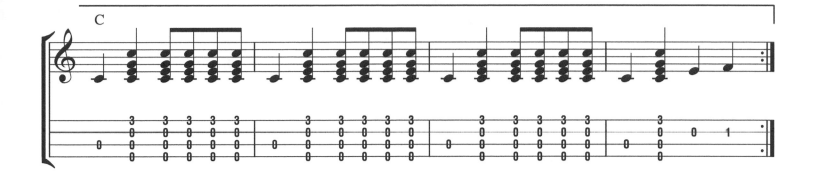

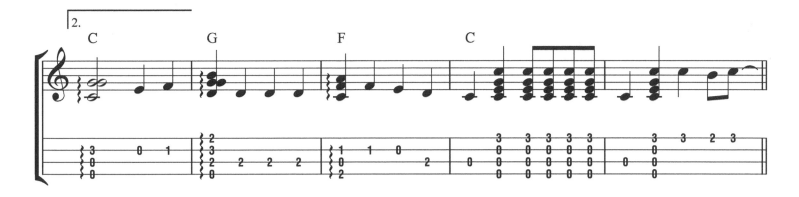

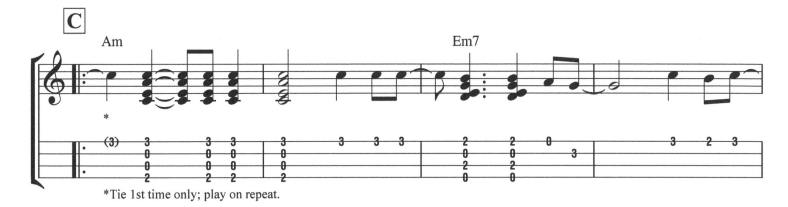

*Tie 1st time only; play on repeat.

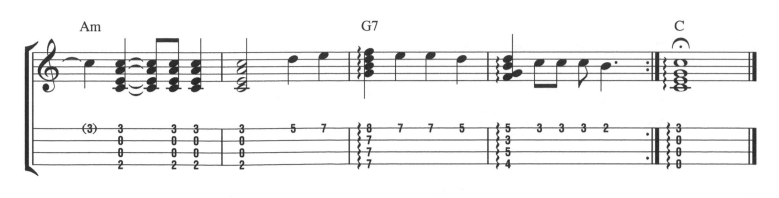

Can't Find My Way Home

Words and Music by Steve Winwood

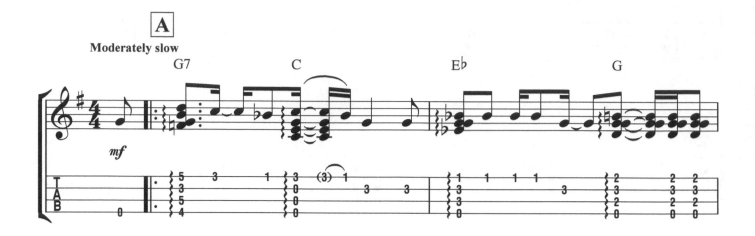

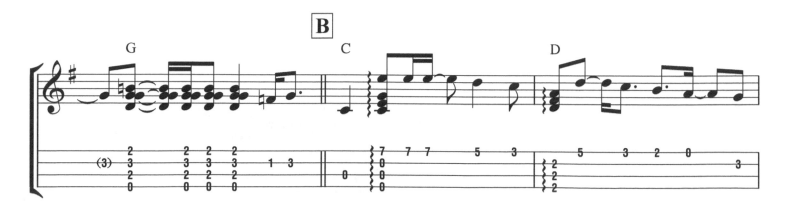

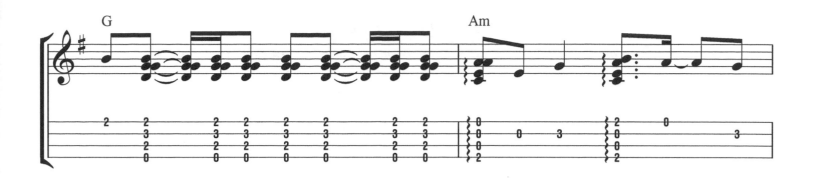

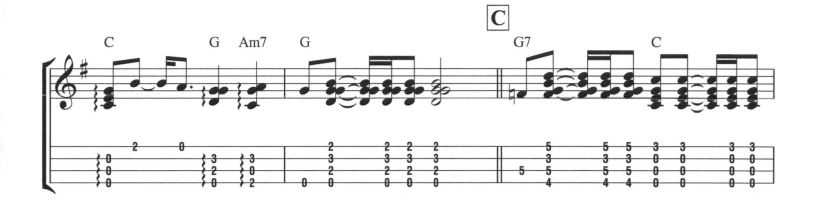

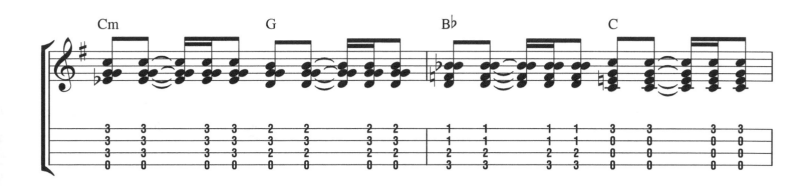

Cavatina

from the Universal Pictures and EMI Films Presentation THE DEER HUNTER

By Stanley Myers

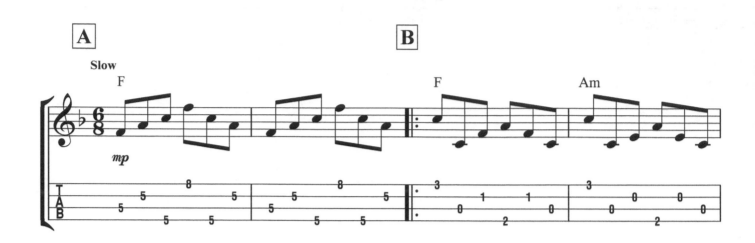

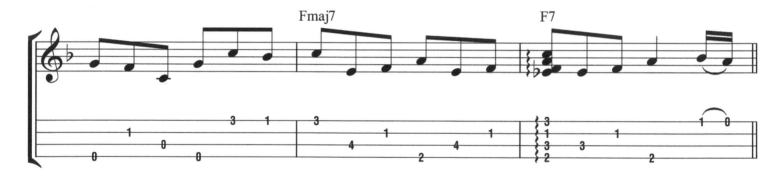

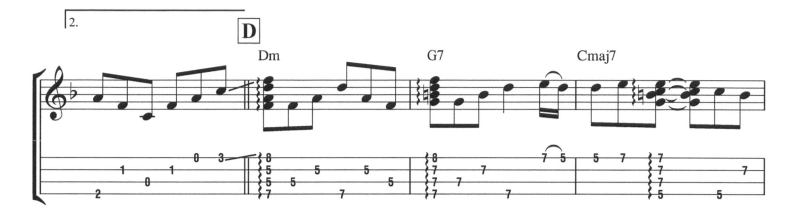

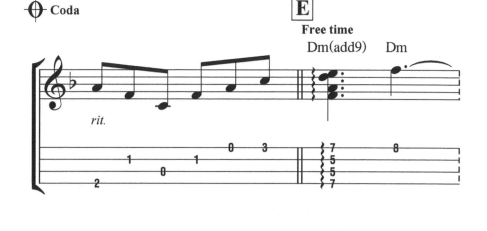

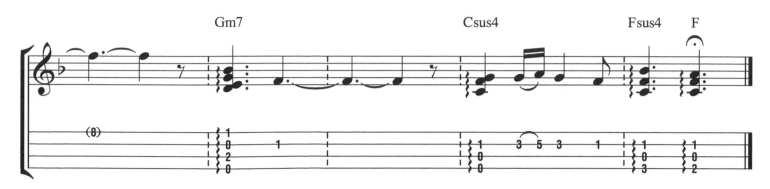

Change the World

Words and Music by Wayne Kirkpatrick, Gordon Kennedy and Tommy Sims

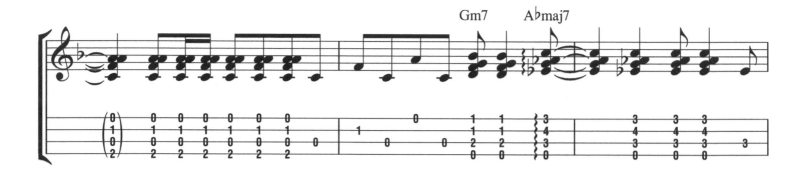

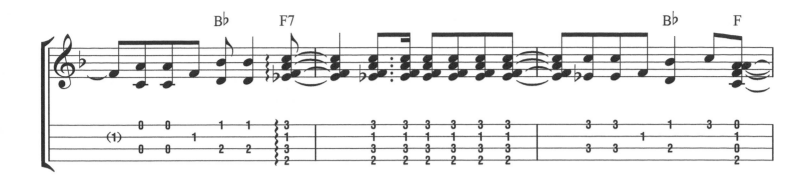

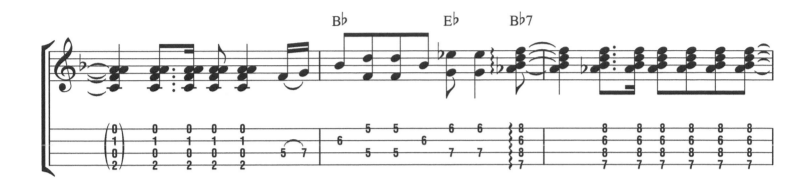

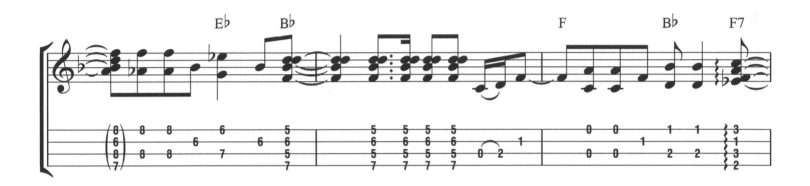

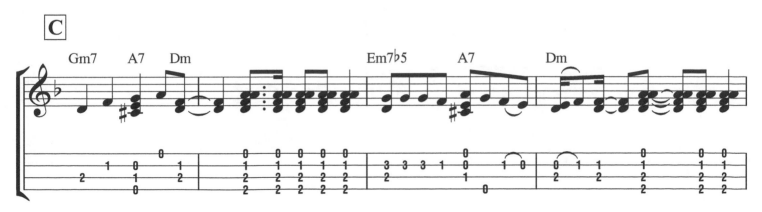

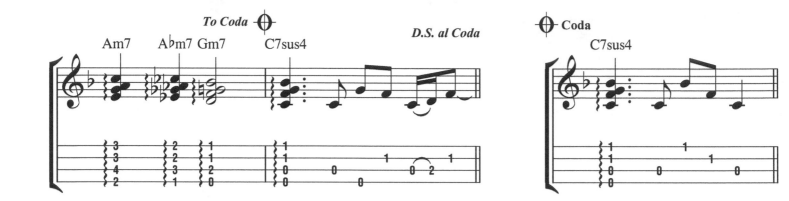

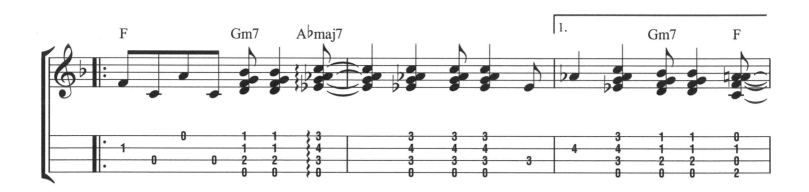

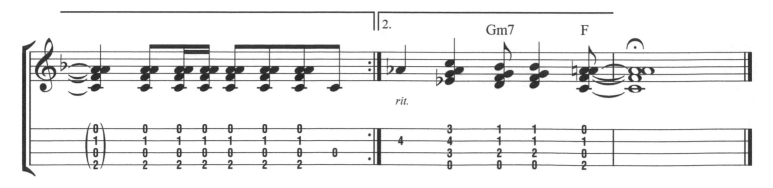

City of Stars

from LA LA LAND

Music by Justin Hurwitz
Lyrics by Benj Pasek & Justin Paul

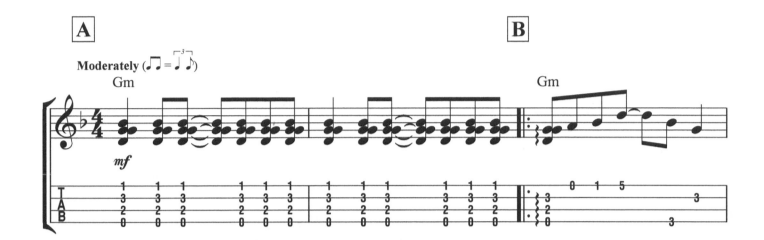

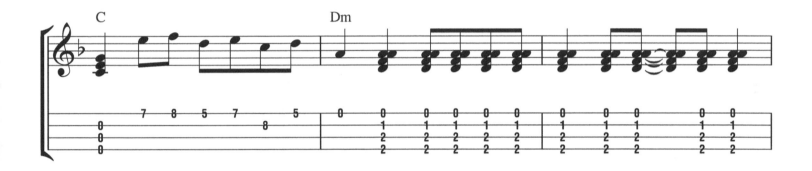

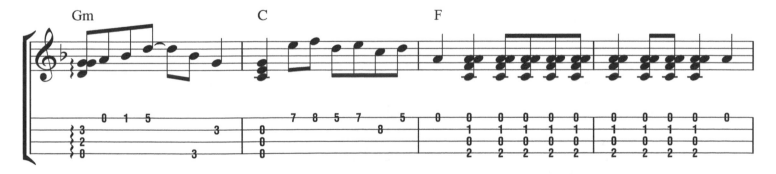

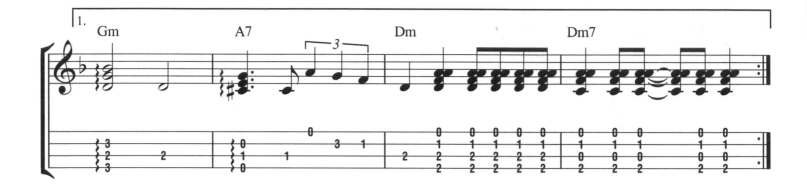

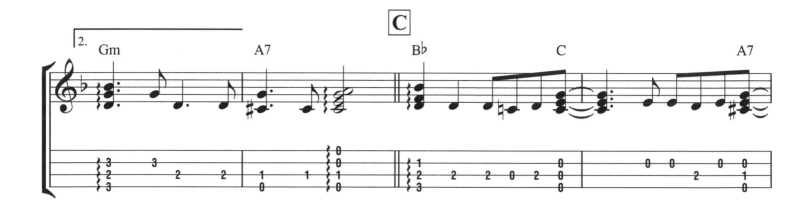

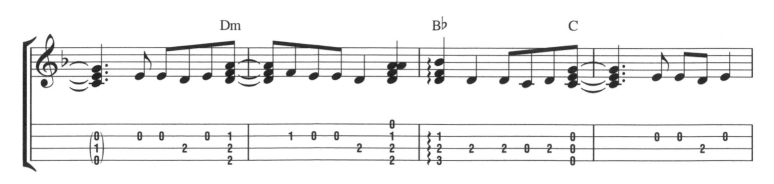

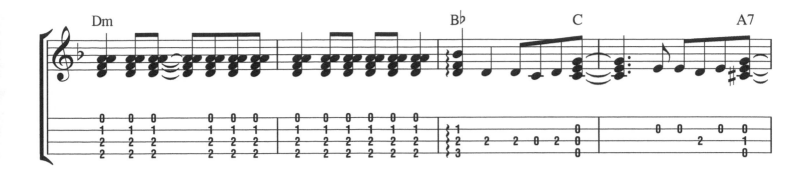

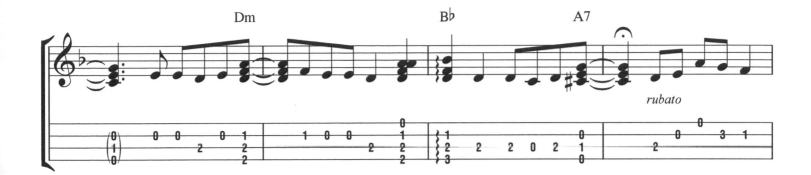

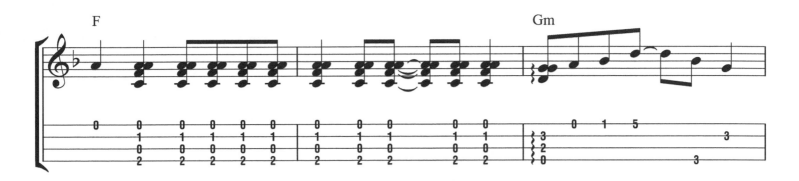

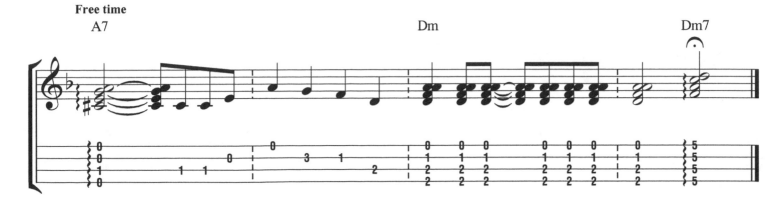

Classical Gas

By Mason Williams

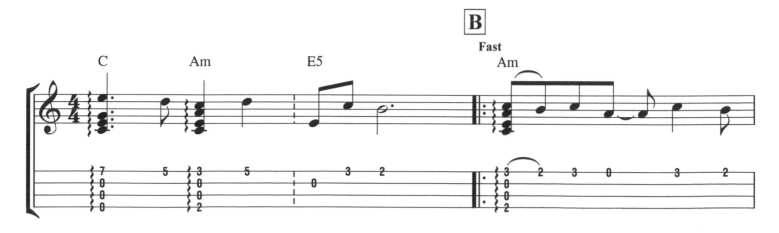

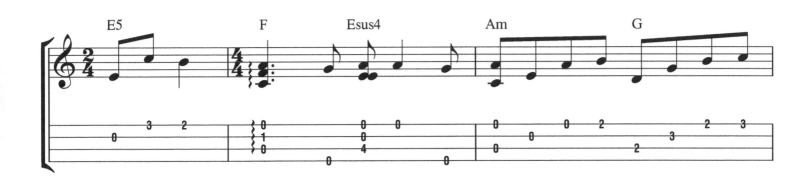

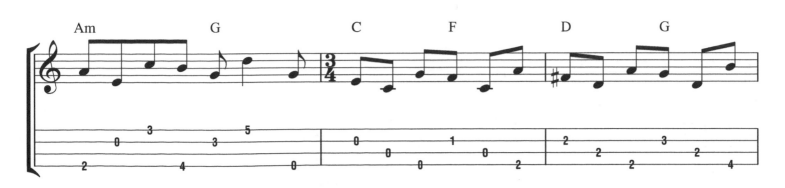

Crazy

Words and Music by Willie Nelson

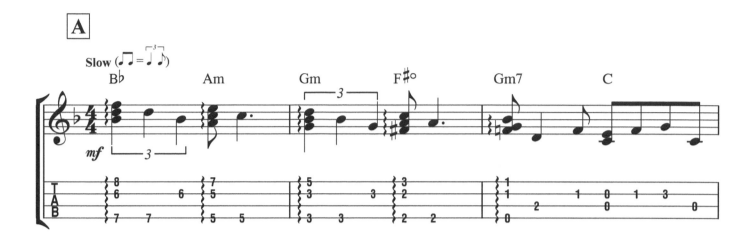

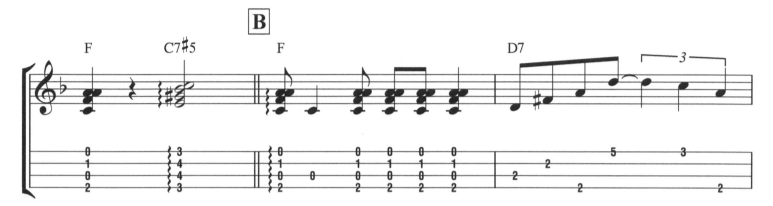

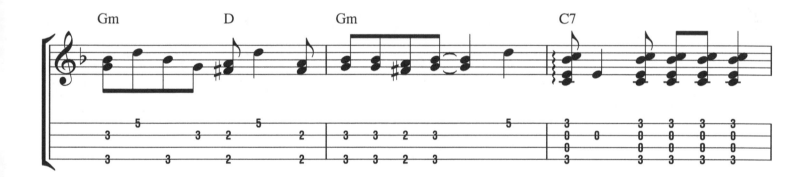

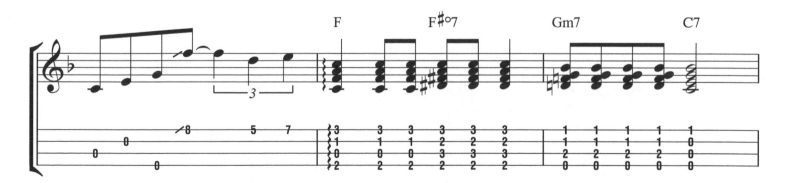

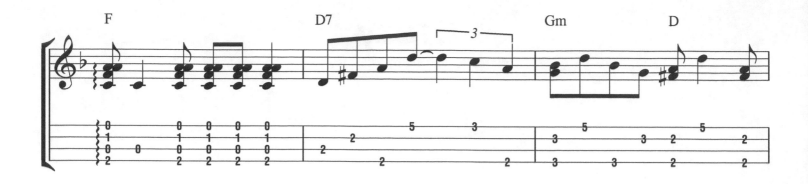

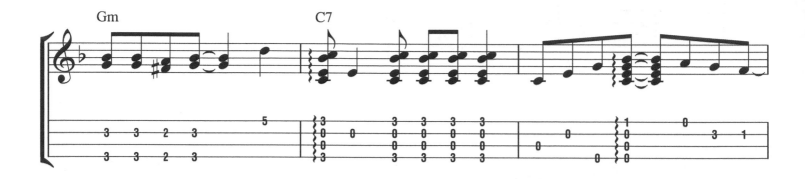

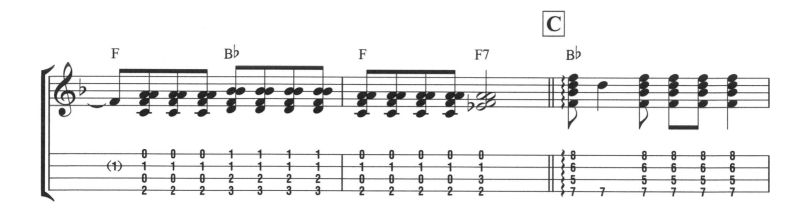

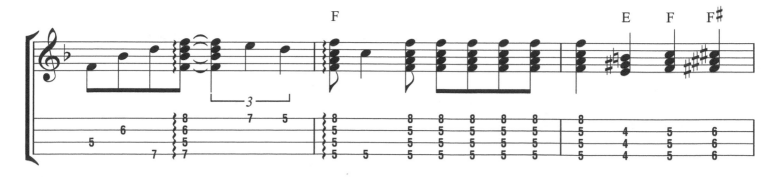

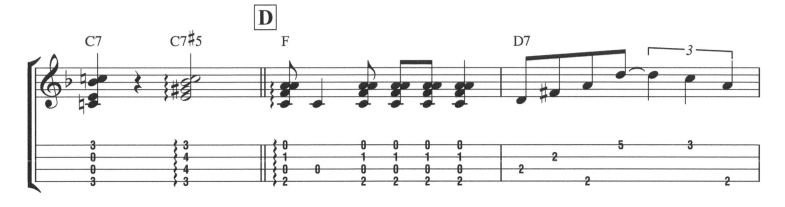

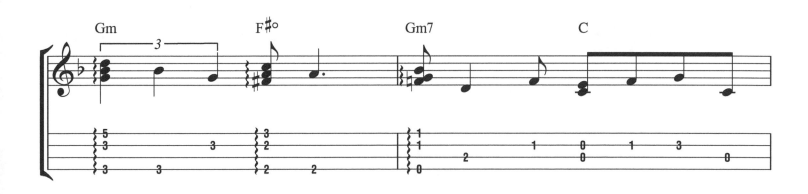

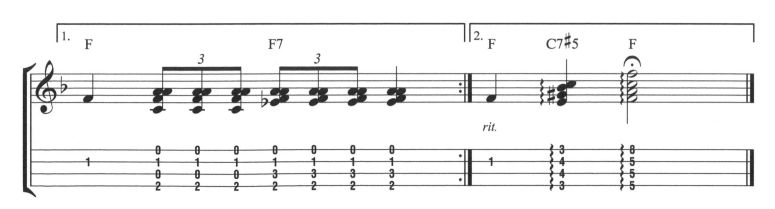

(They Long to Be) Close to You

Lyrics by Hal David
Music by Burt Bacharach

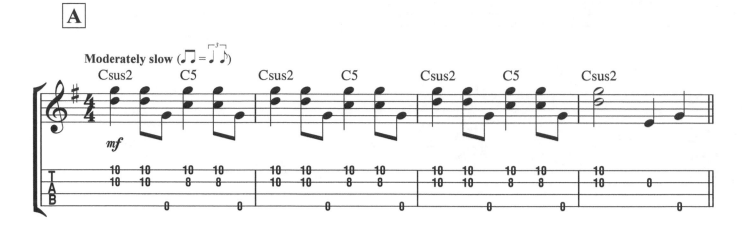

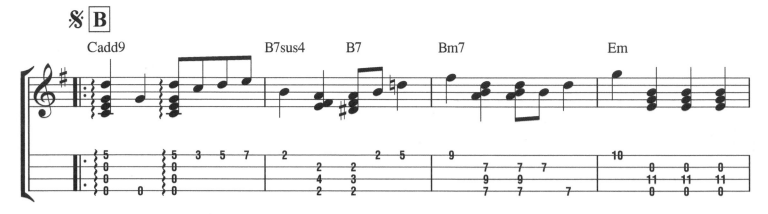

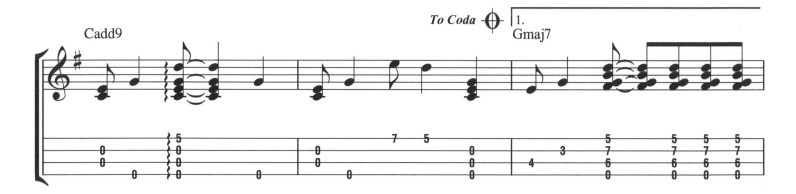

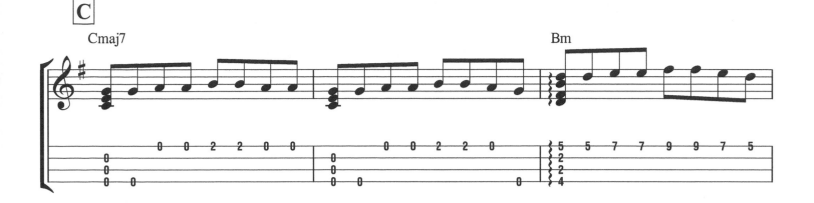

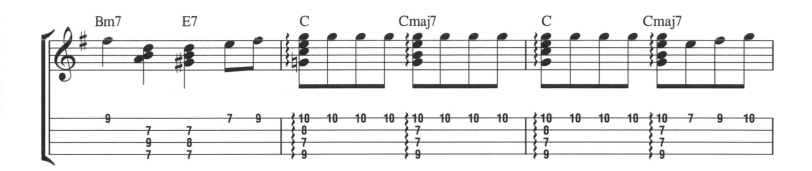

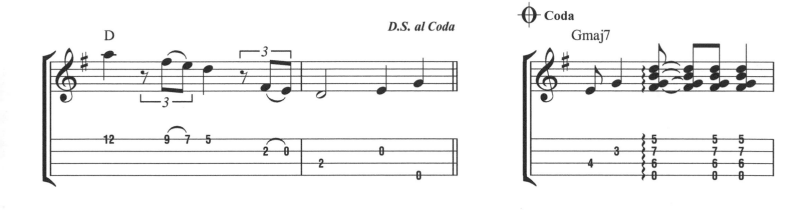

Dream a Little Dream of Me

Words by Gus Kahn
Music by Wilbur Schwandt and Fabian Andree

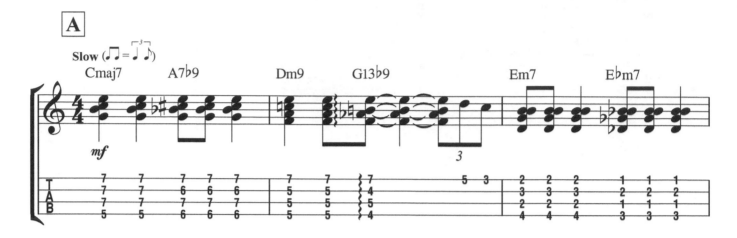

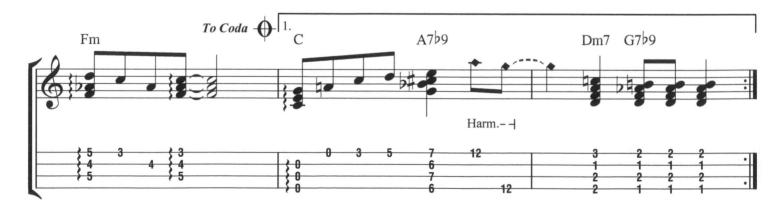

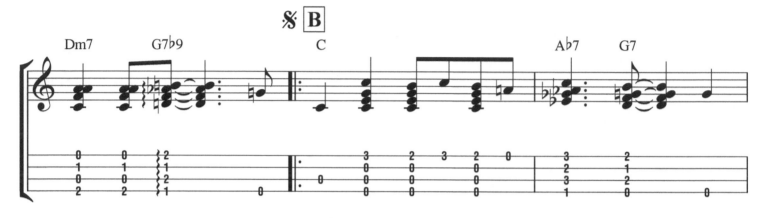

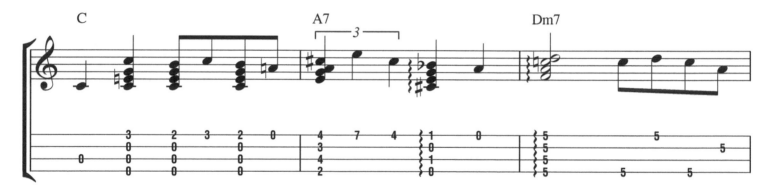

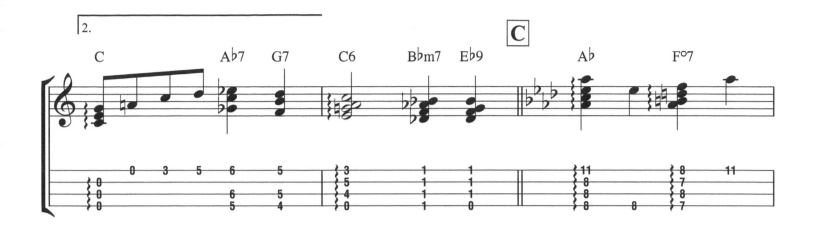

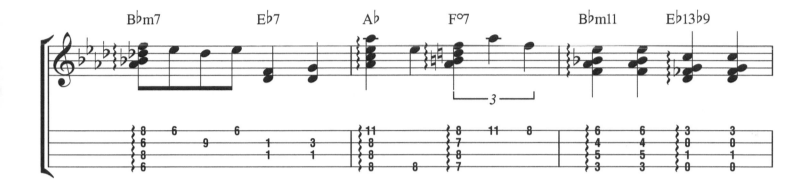

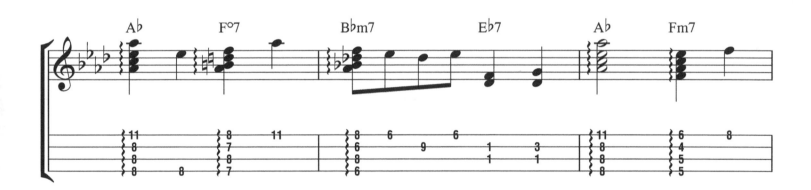

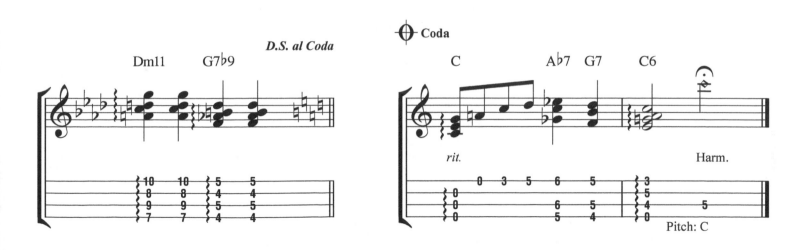

Dust in the Wind

Words and Music by Kerry Livgren

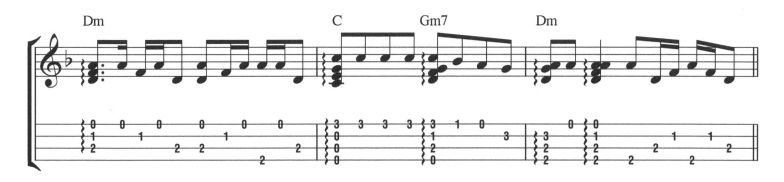

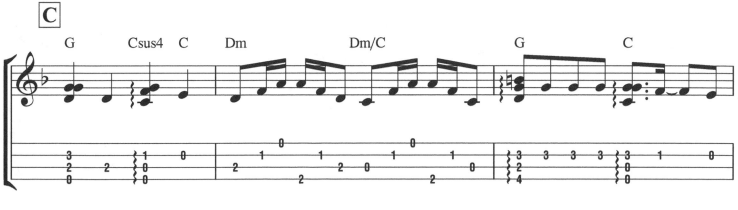

Every Breath You Take

Music and Lyrics by Sting

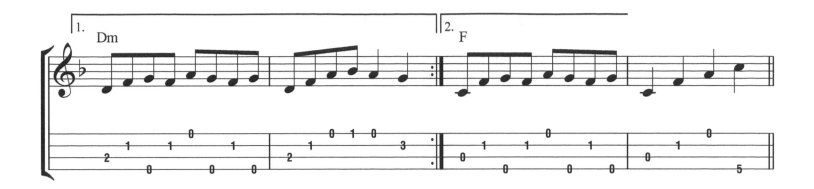

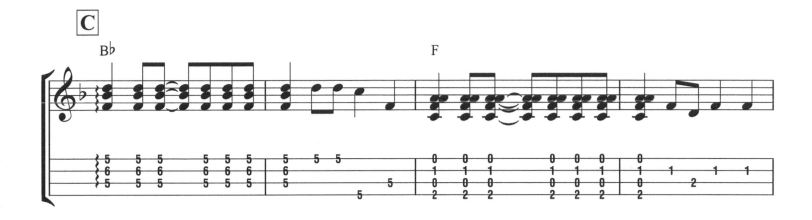

C

D.S. al Coda

Coda

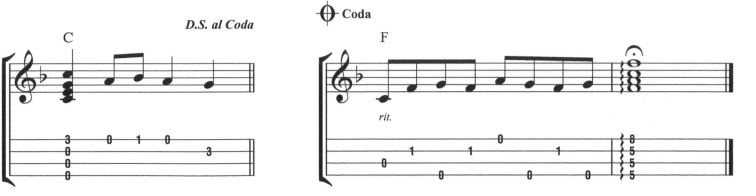

49

Fire and Rain

Words and Music by James Taylor

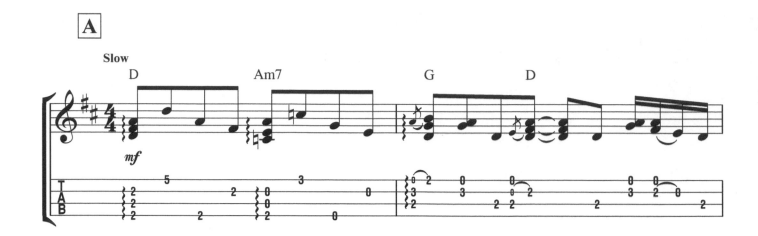

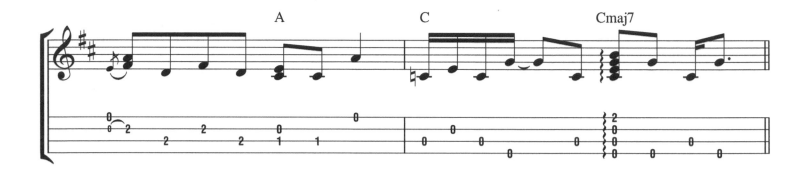

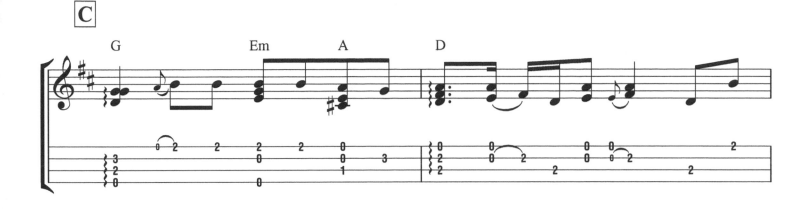

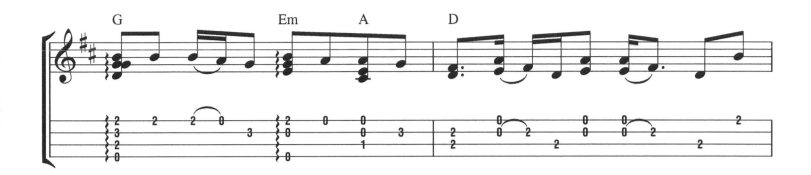

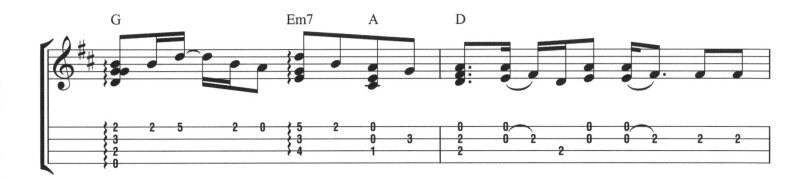

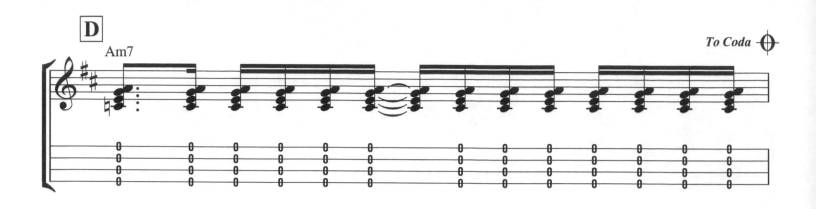

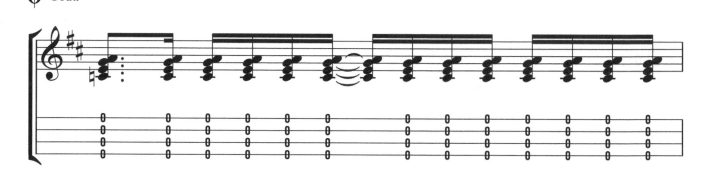

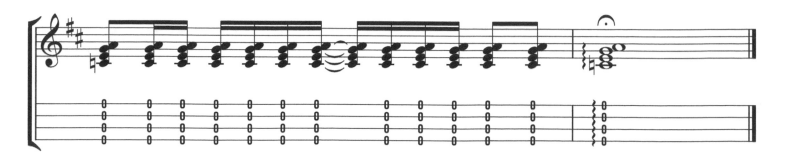

Happy Birthday to You

Words and Music by Mildred J. Hill and Patty S. Hill

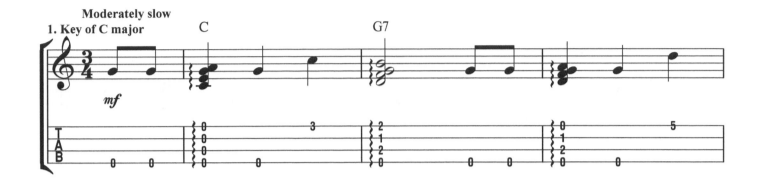

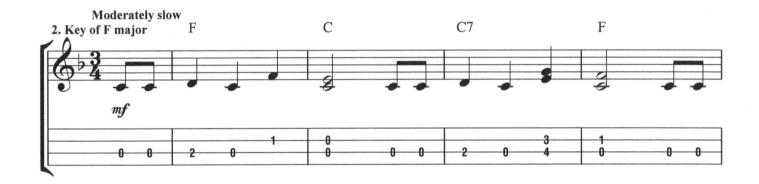

53

Fly Me to the Moon
(In Other Words)

Words and Music by Bart Howard

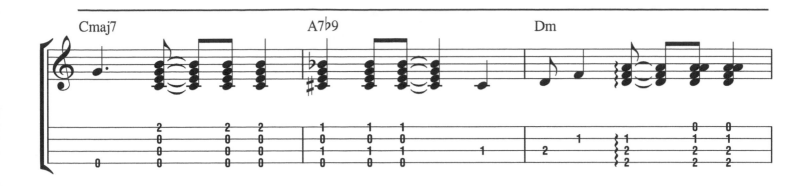

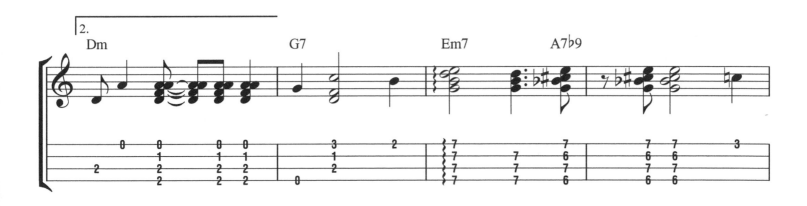

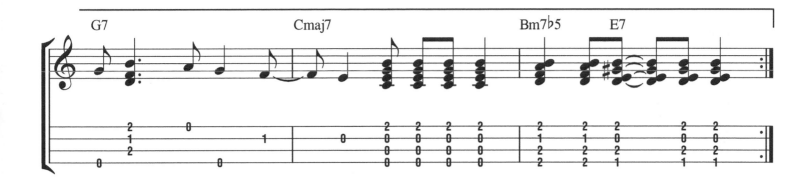

Freight Train

Words and Music by Elizabeth Cotten

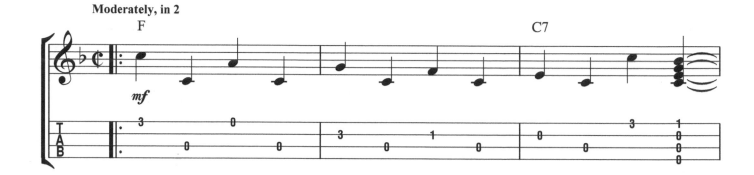

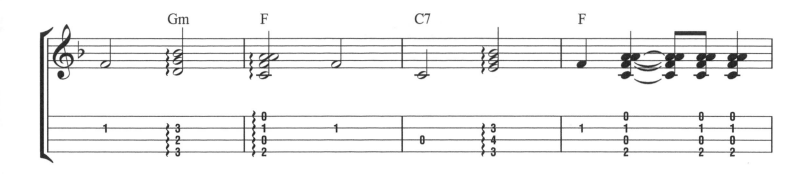

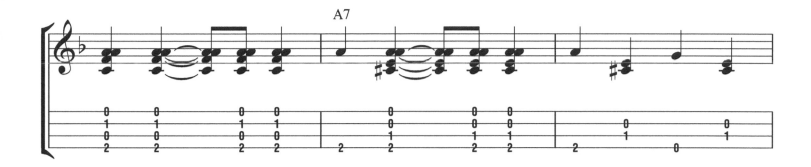

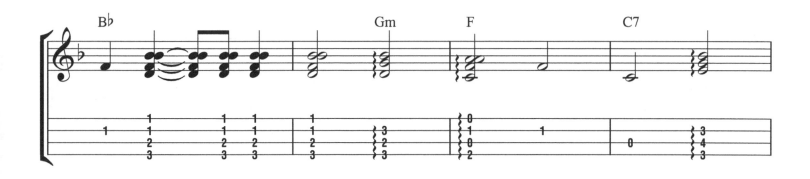

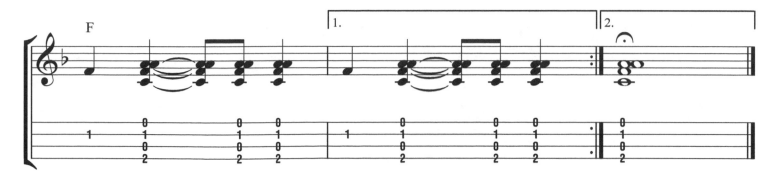

Für Elise
WoO 59
By Ludwig van Beethoven

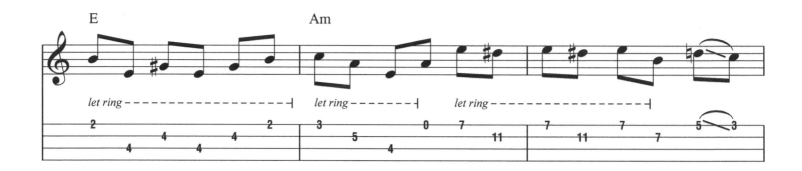

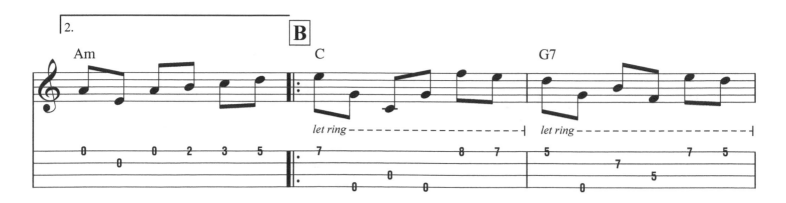

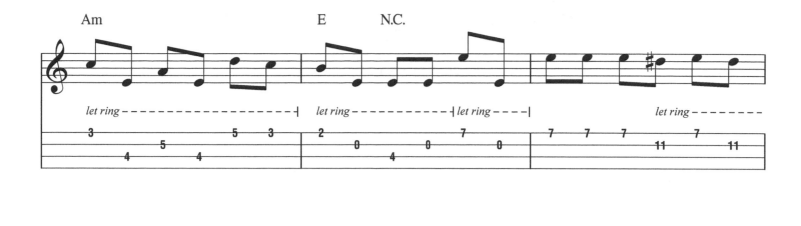

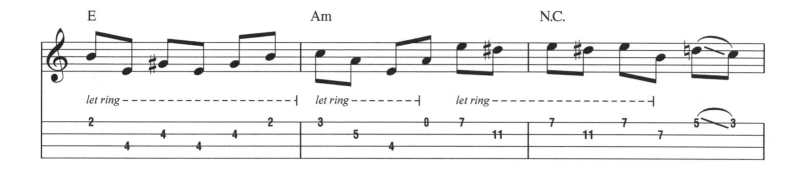

Georgia on My Mind

Words by Stuart Gorrell
Music by Hoagy Carmichael

A

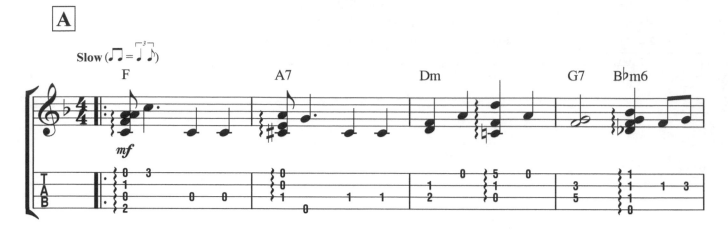

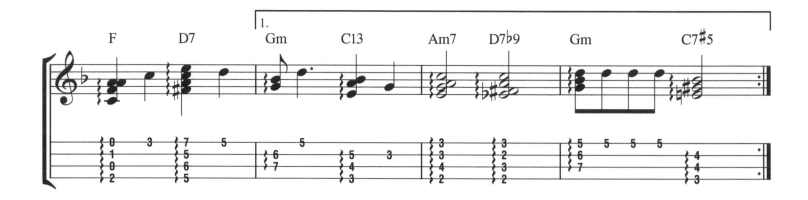

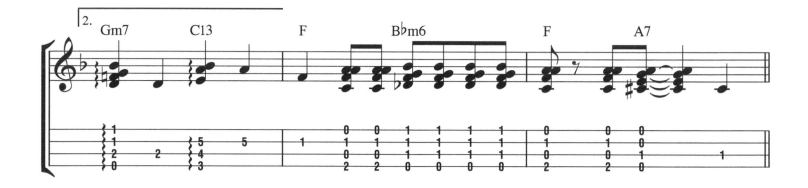

B

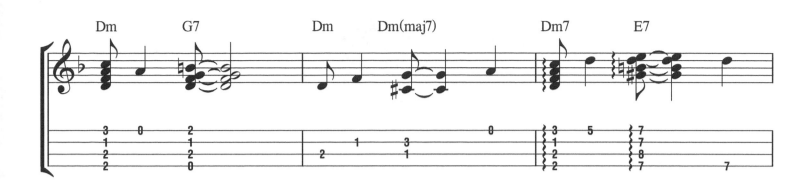

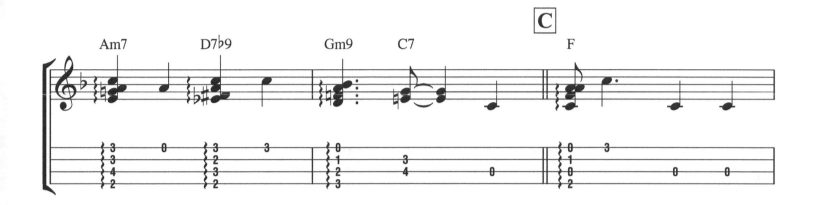

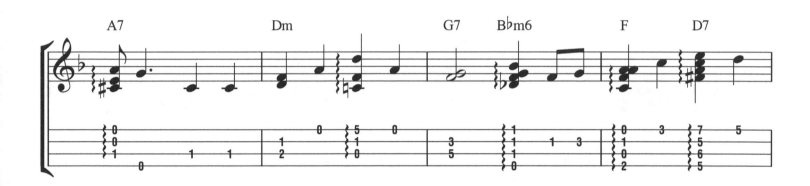

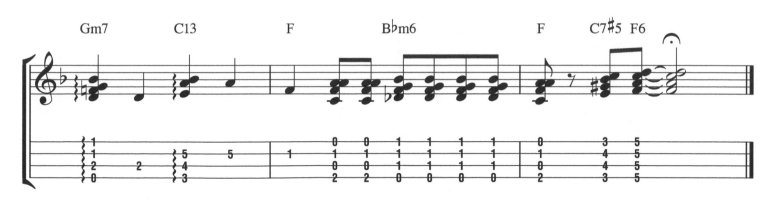

The Godfather

(Love Theme)

from the Paramount Picture THE GODFATHER

By Nino Rota

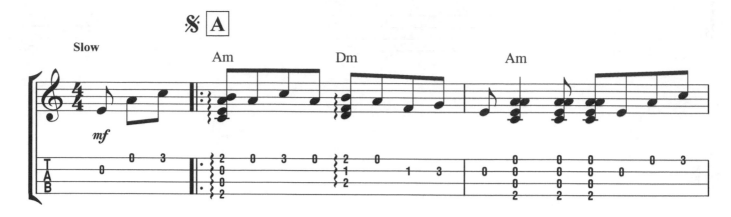

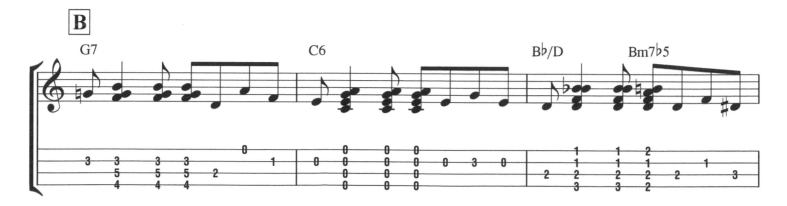

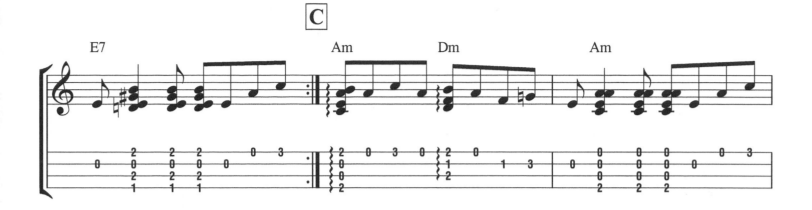

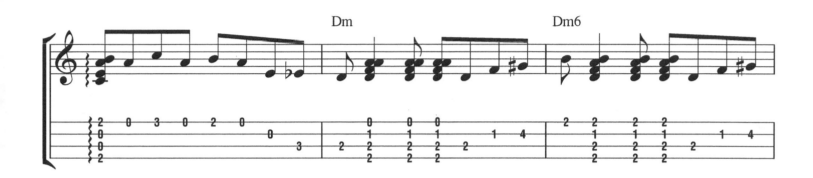

Helplessly Hoping

Words and Music by Stephen Stills

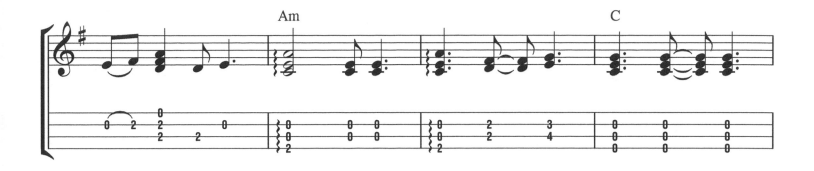

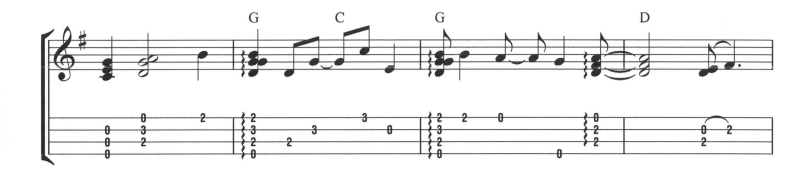

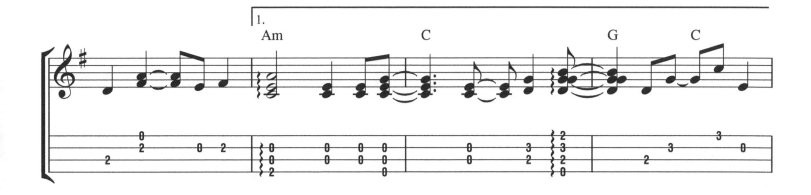

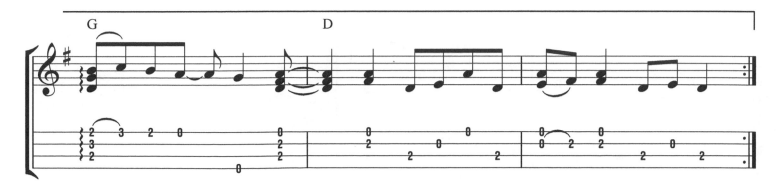

Jamaica Farewell

Words and Music by Irving Burgie

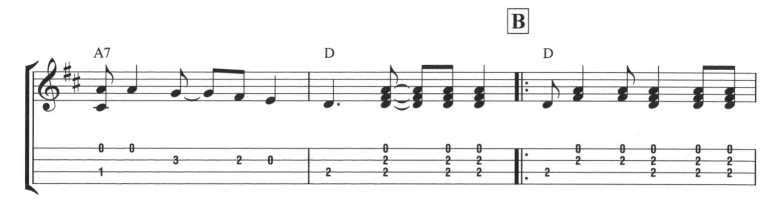

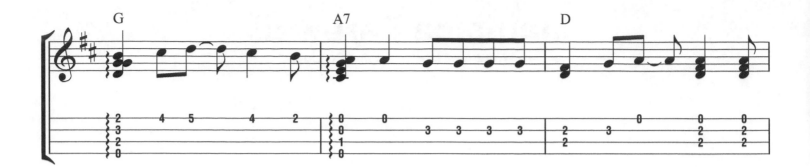

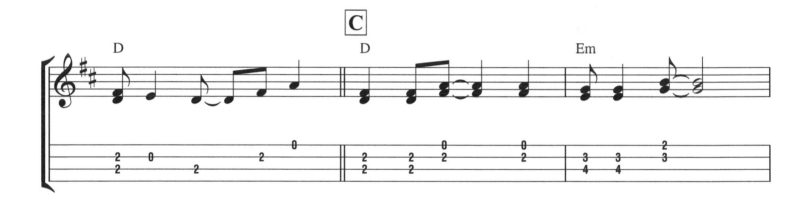

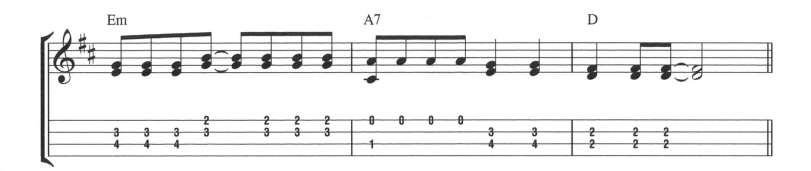

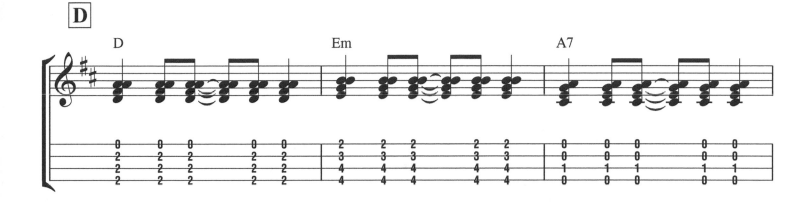

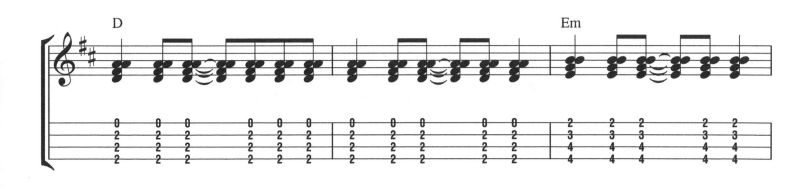

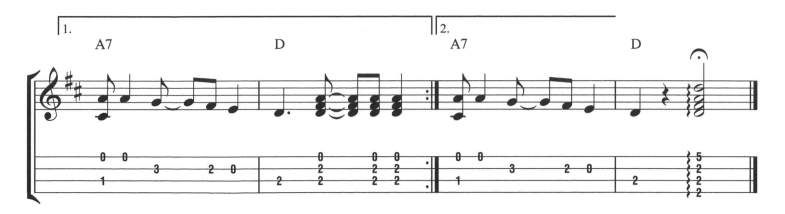

Hopelessly Devoted to You

from GREASE

Words and Music by John Farrar

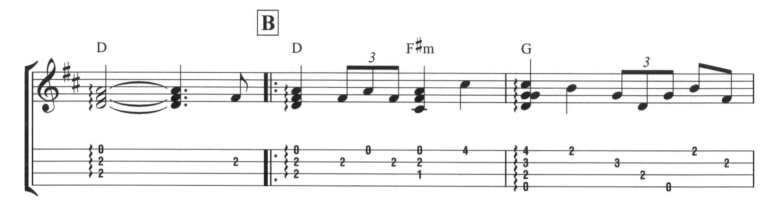

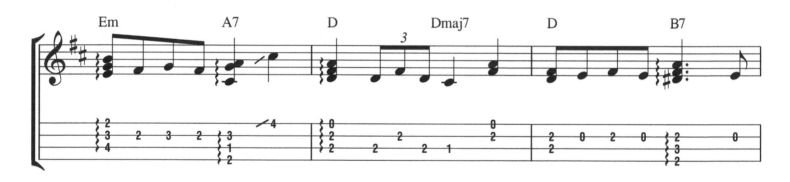

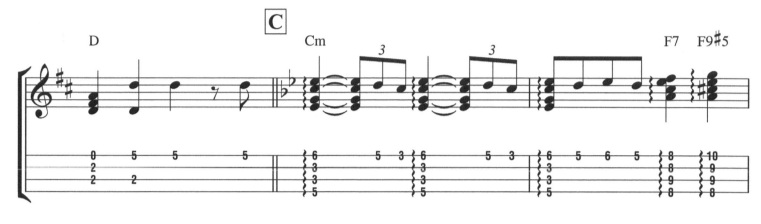

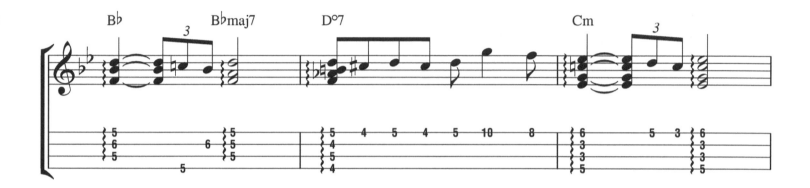

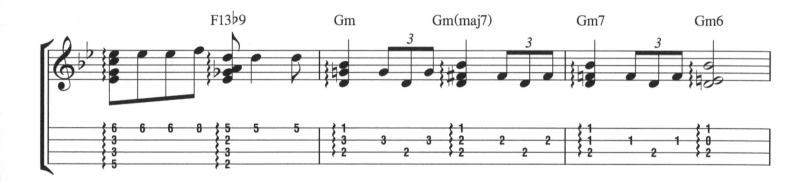

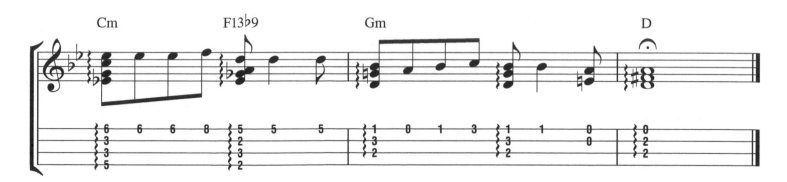

I'm Yours

Words and Music by Jason Mraz

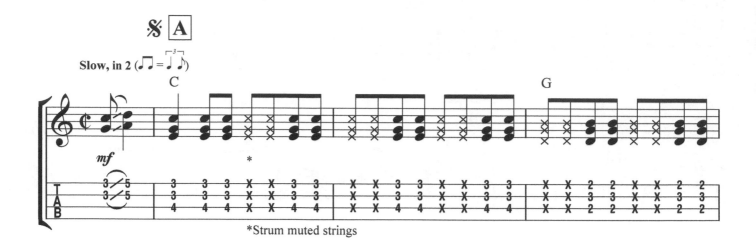

*Strum muted strings

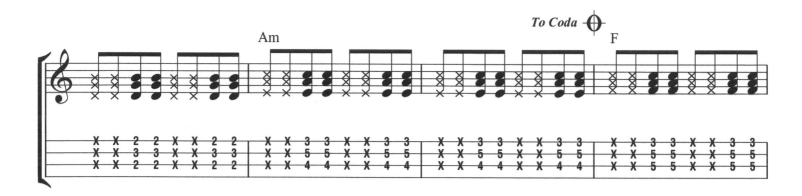

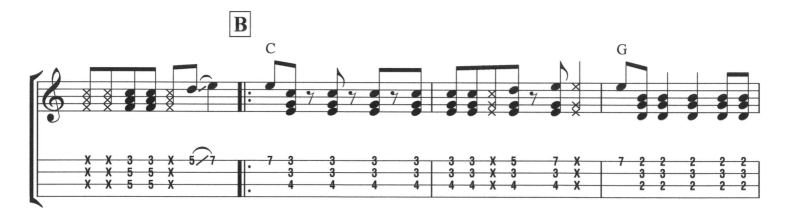

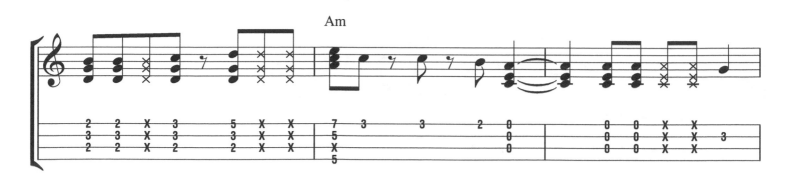

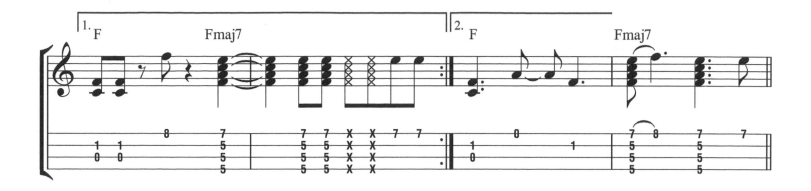

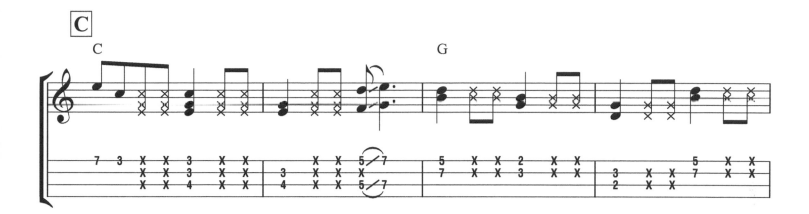

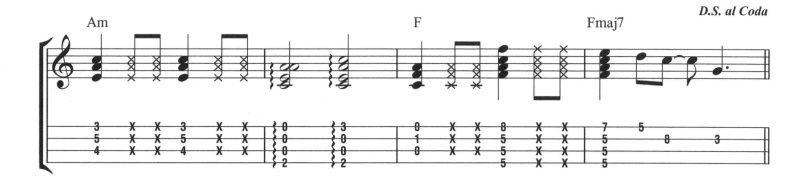

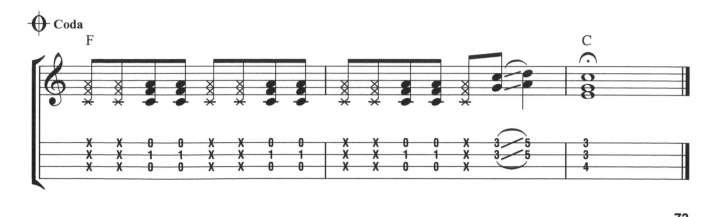

Imagine

Words and Music by John Lennon

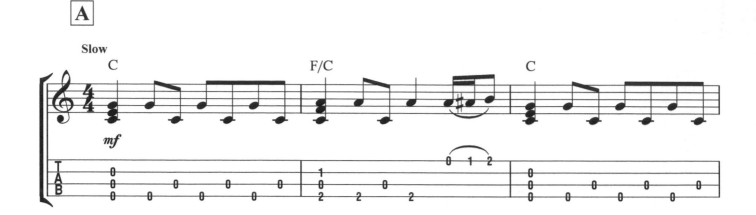

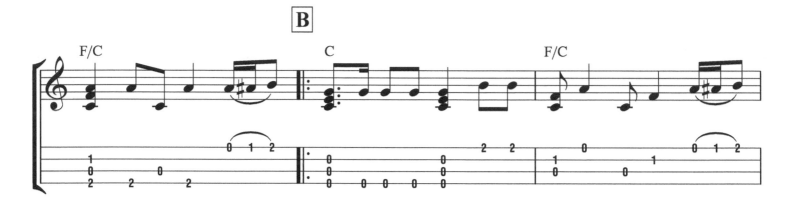

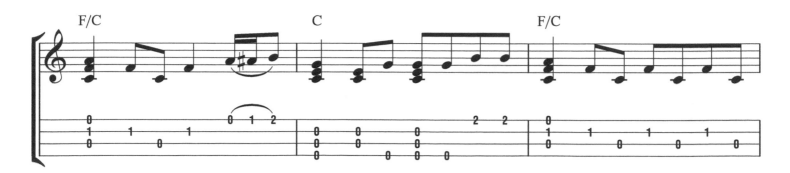

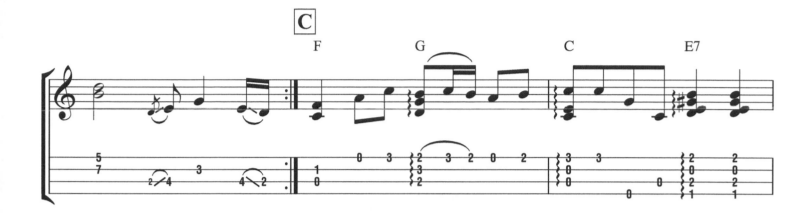

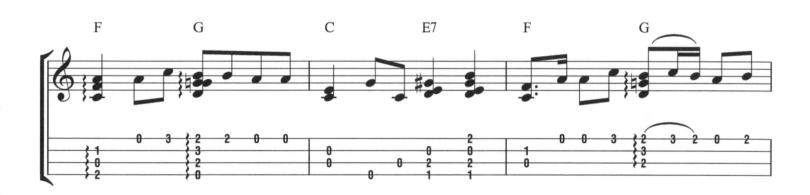

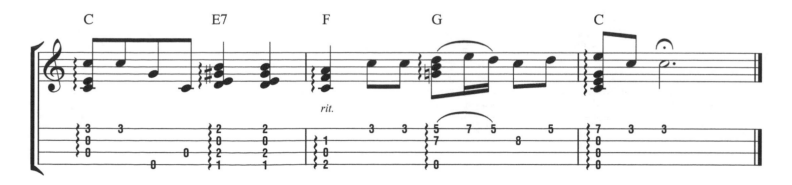

In My Life

Words and Music by John Lennon and Paul McCartney

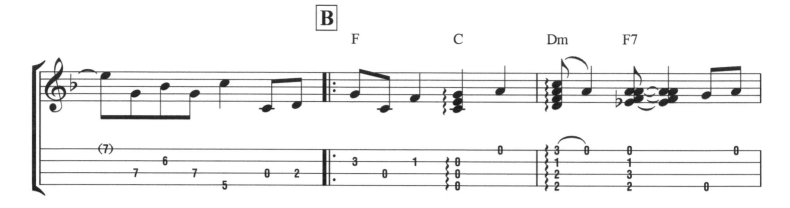

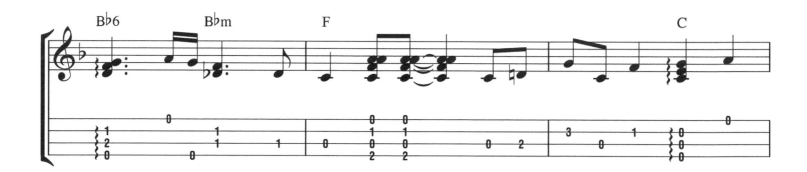

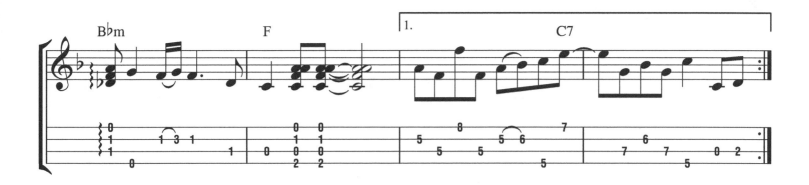

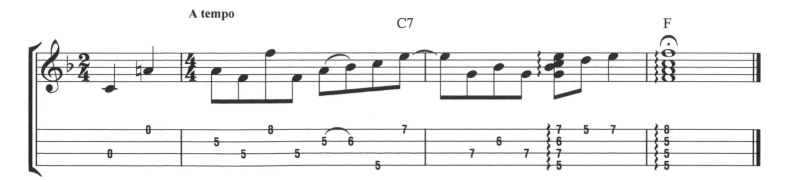

Isn't She Lovely

Words and Music by Stevie Wonder

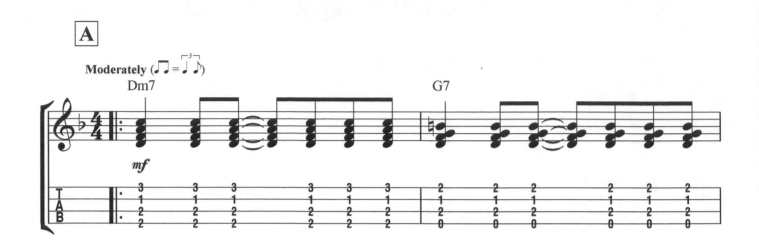

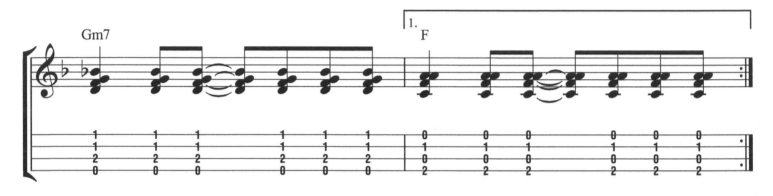

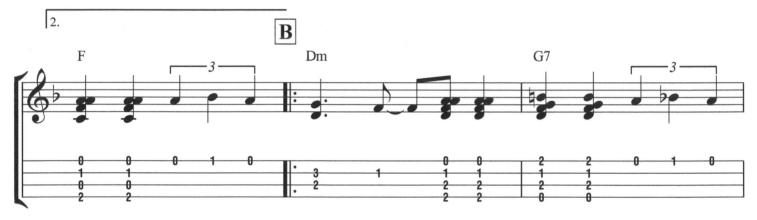

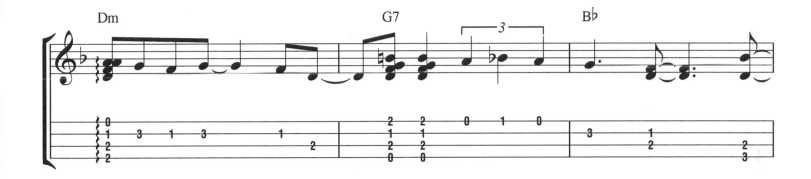

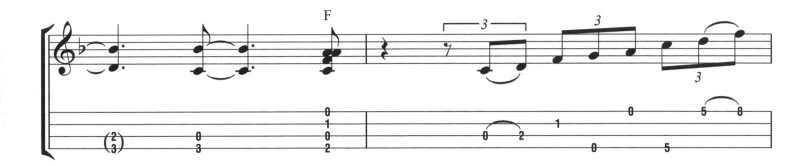

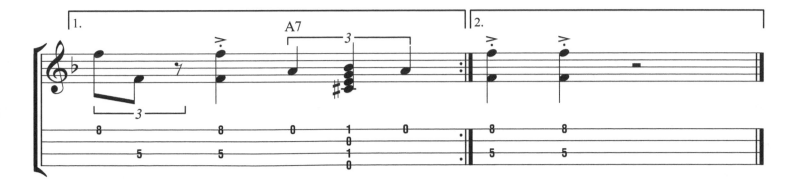

Kiss from a Rose

Words and Music by Henry Olusegun Adeola Samuel

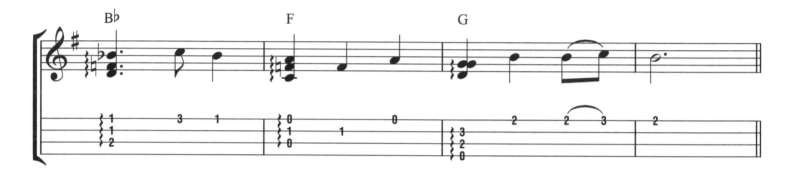

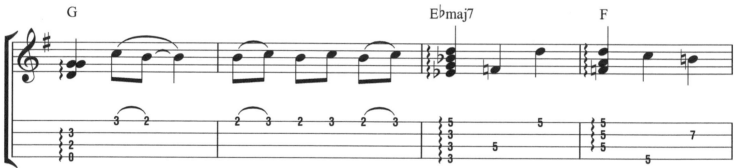

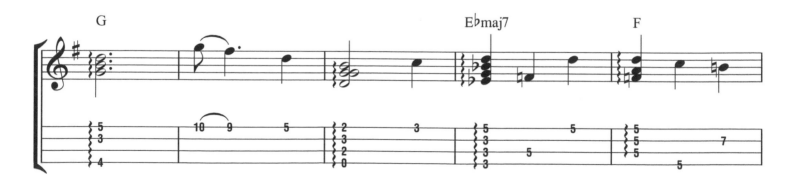

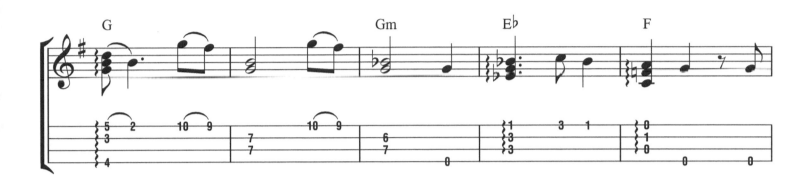

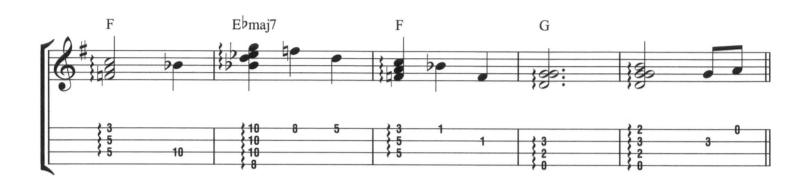

D

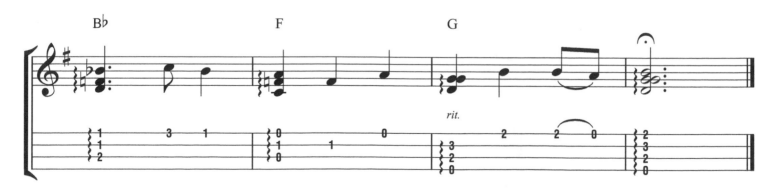

Leyenda

By Isaac Albeniz

Tuning: ↓G-C-E-A

Moderately

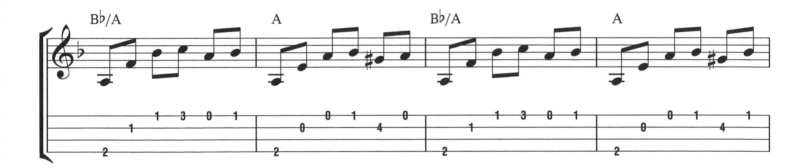

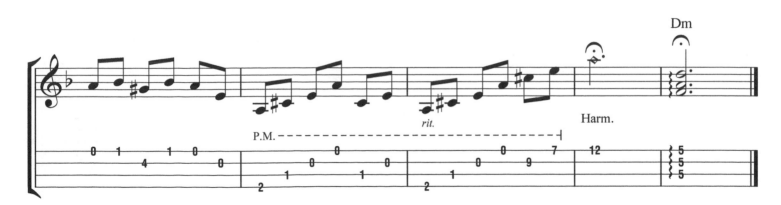

A Million Dreams

from THE GREATEST SHOWMAN

Words and Music by Benj Pasek and Justin Paul

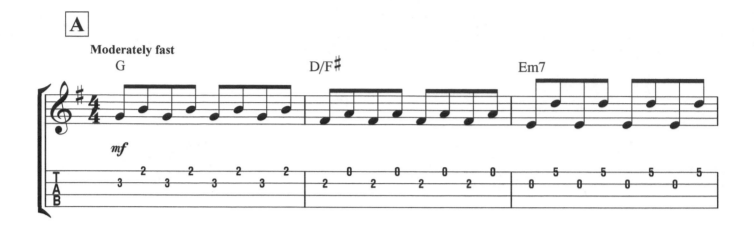

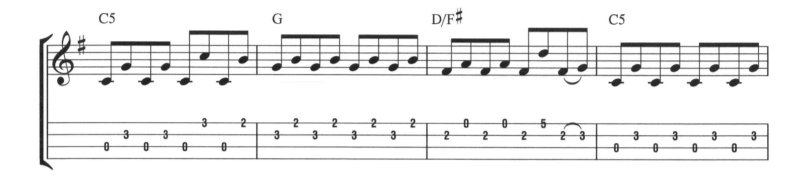

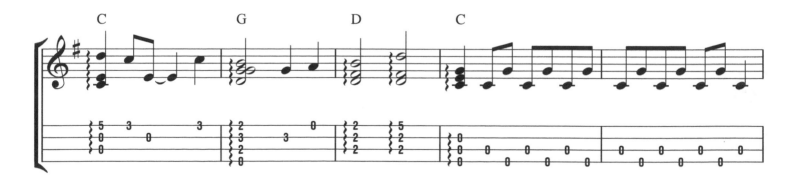

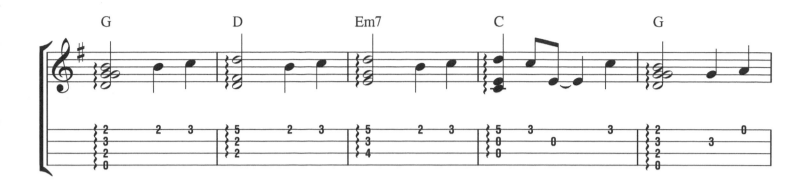

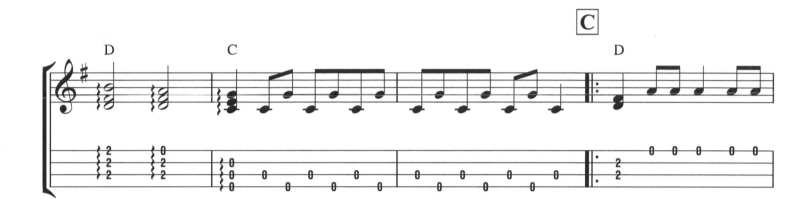

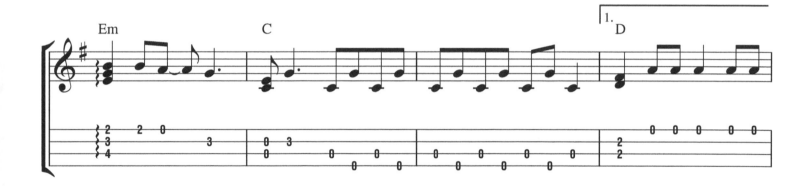

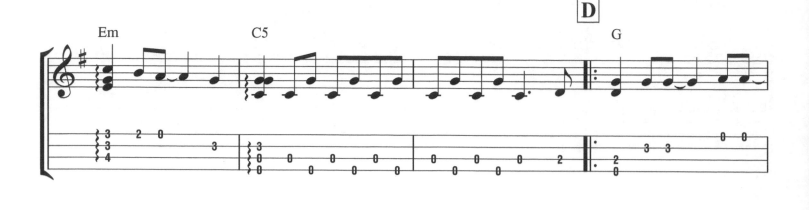

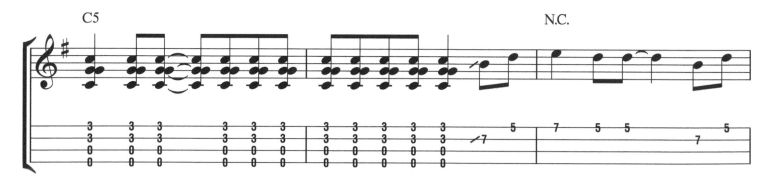

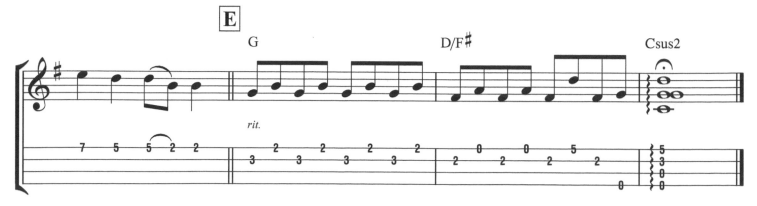

Perfect

Words and Music by Ed Sheeran

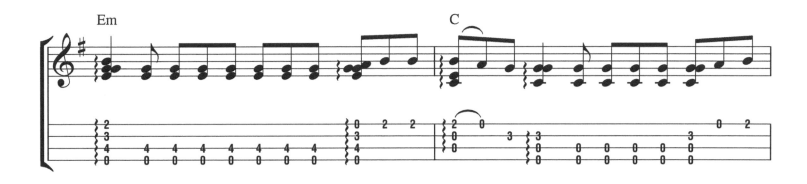

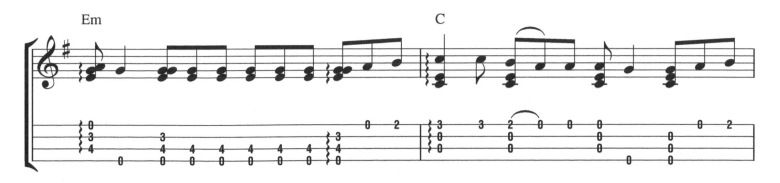

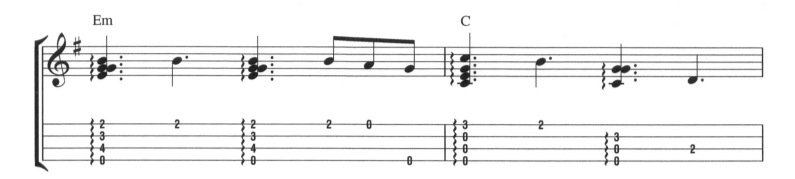

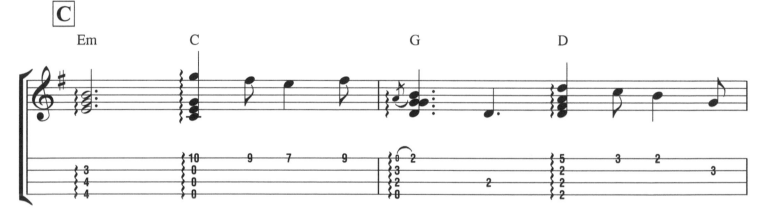

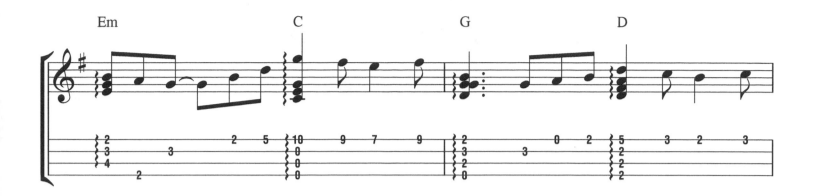

D.S. al Coda
(take repeat)

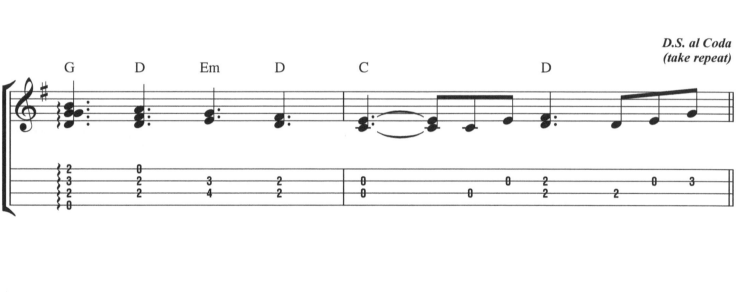

⊕ **Coda**

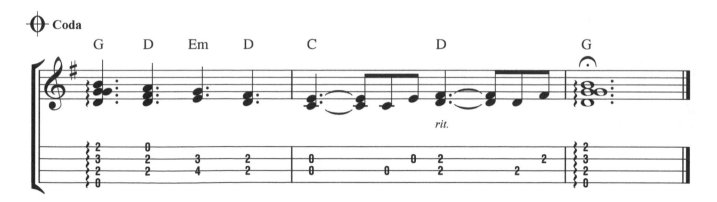

rit.

My Funny Valentine

from BABES IN ARMS
Words by Lorenz Hart
Music by Richard Rodgers

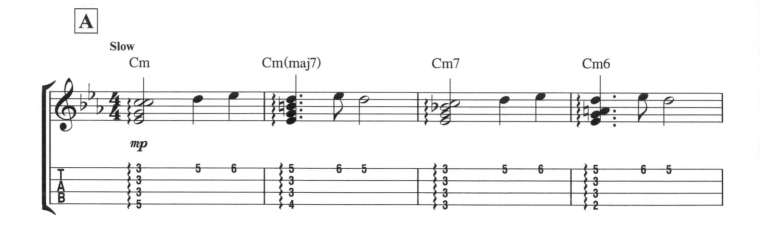

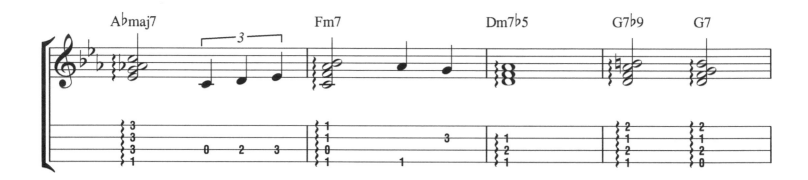

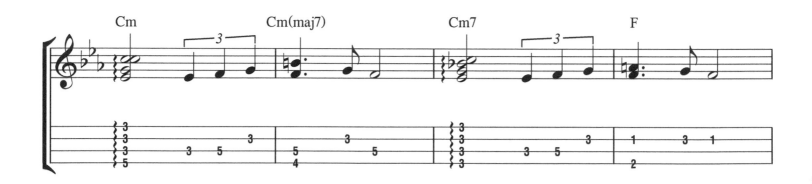

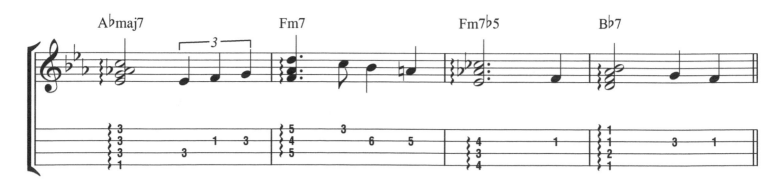

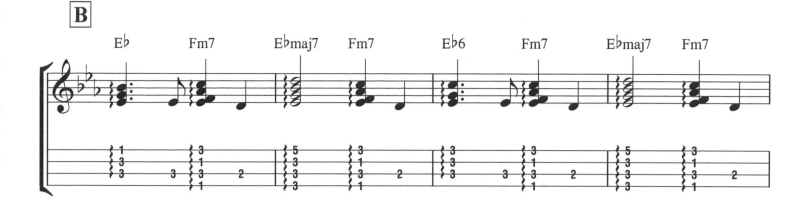

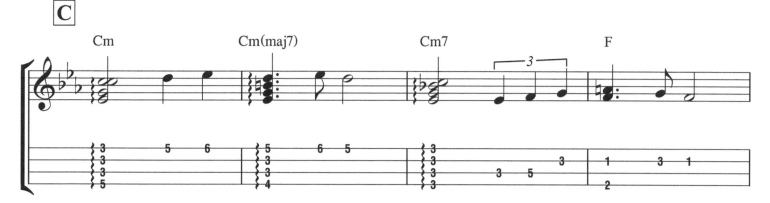

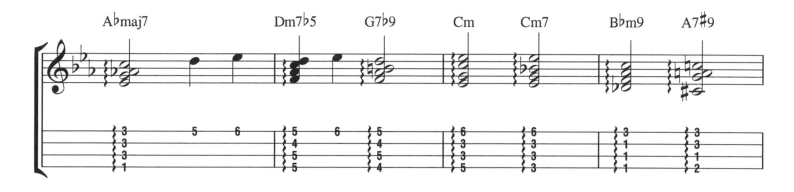

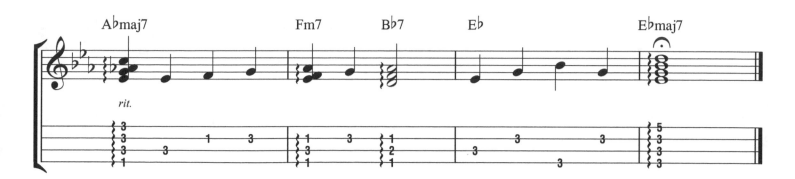

Never Going Back Again

Words and Music by Lindsey Buckingham

To Coda ⊕

D.S. al Coda
(take repeat)

⊕ **Coda**

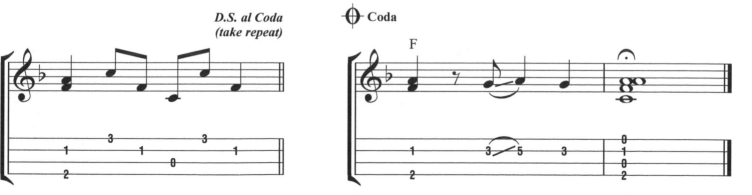

No Woman No Cry

Words and Music by Vincent Ford

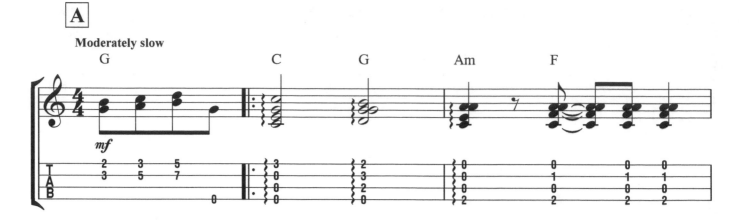

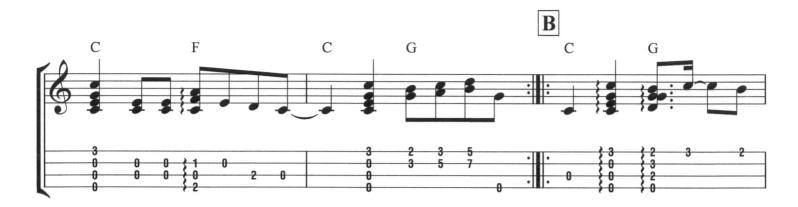

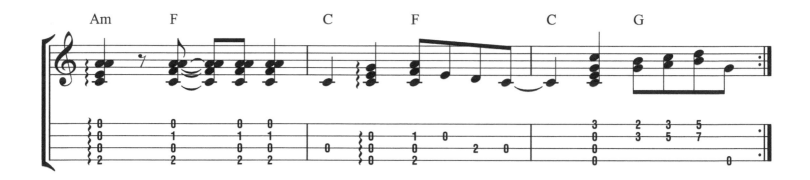

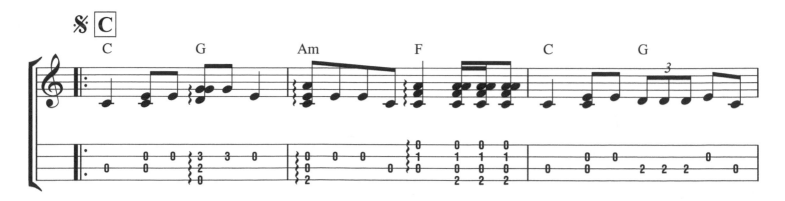

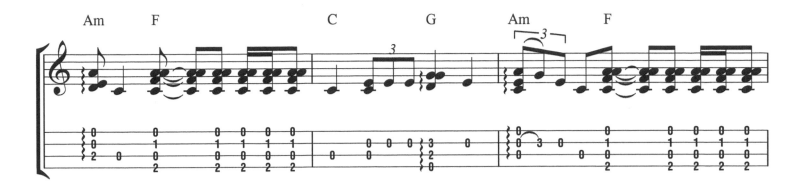

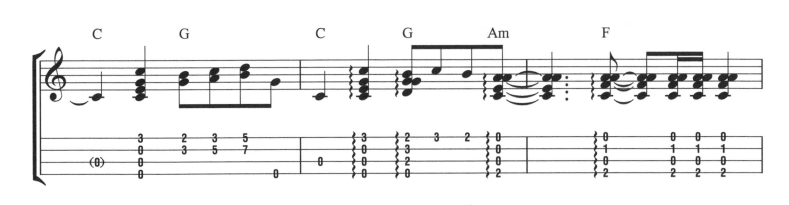

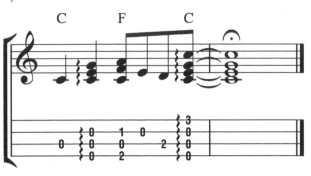

People Get Ready

Words and Music by Curtis Mayfield

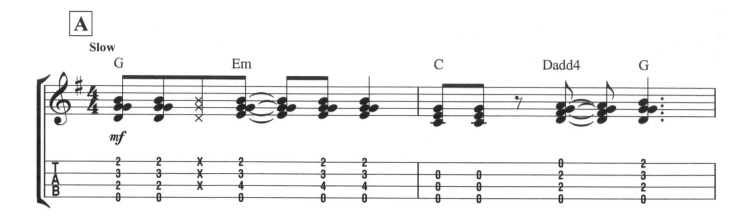

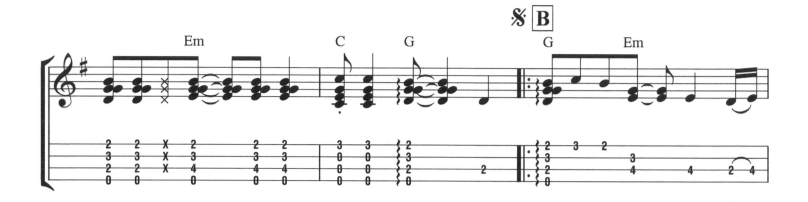

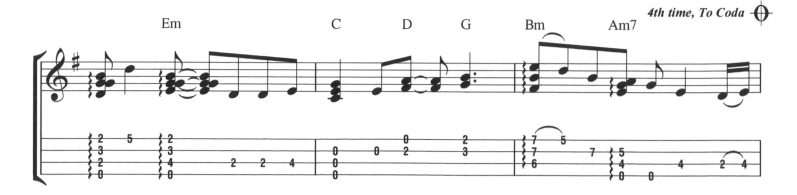

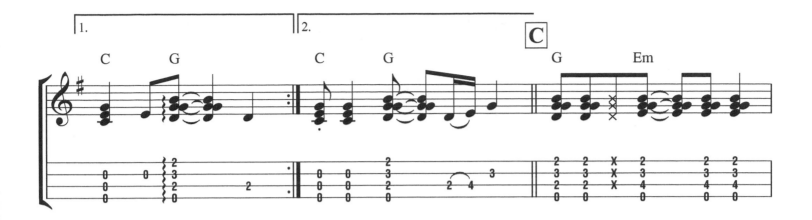

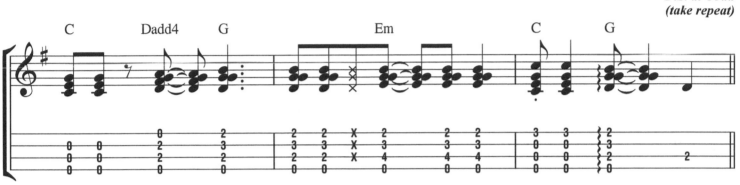

D.S. al Coda
(take repeat)

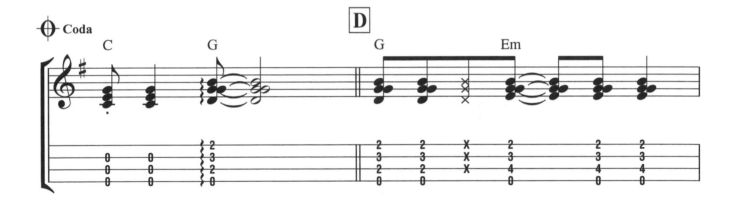

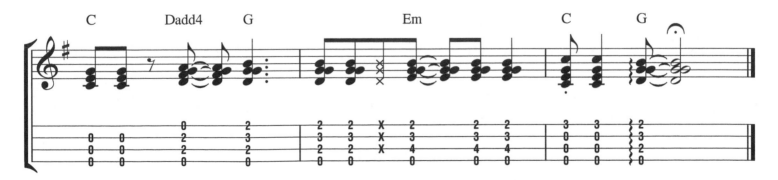

Silent Night

Words by Joseph Mohr
Translated by John F. Young
Music by Franz X. Gruber

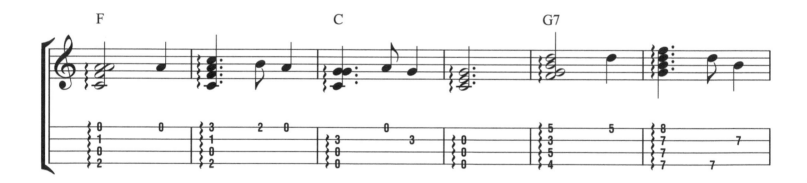

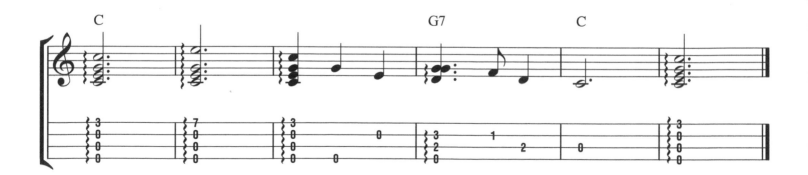

Stand by Me

Words and Music by Jerry Leiber, Mike Stoller and Ben E. King

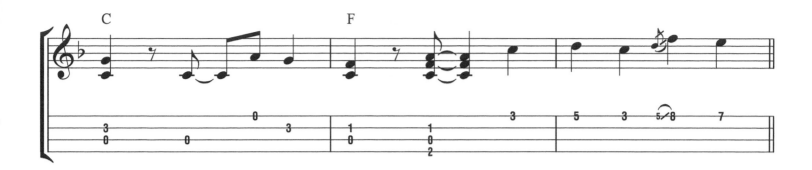

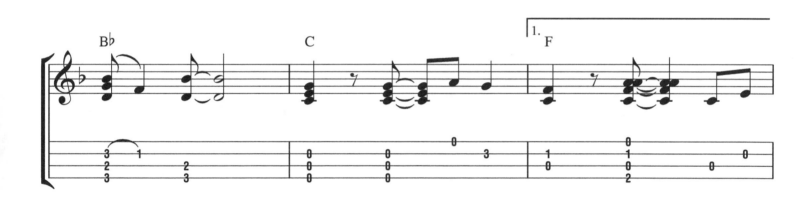

Summertime

from PORGY AND BESS ®

Music and Lyrics by George Gershwin, DuBose and Dorothy Heyward and Ira Gershwin

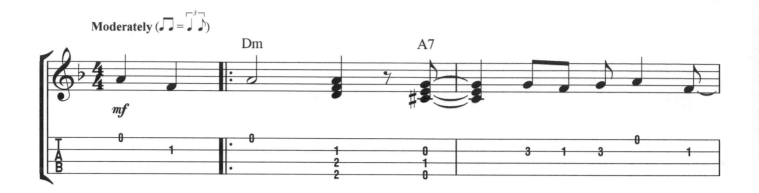

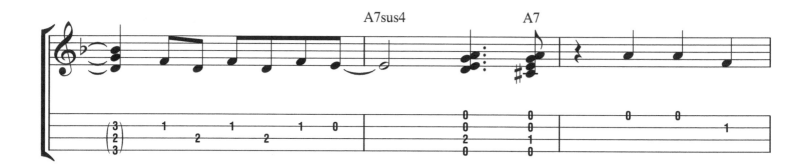

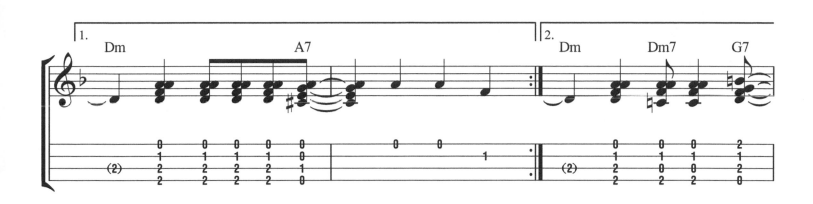

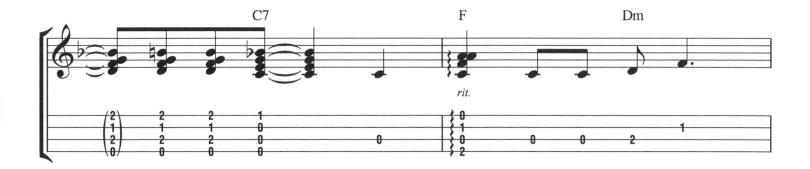

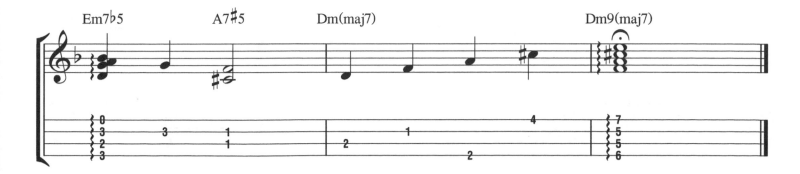

Time in a Bottle

Words and Music by Jim Croce

A

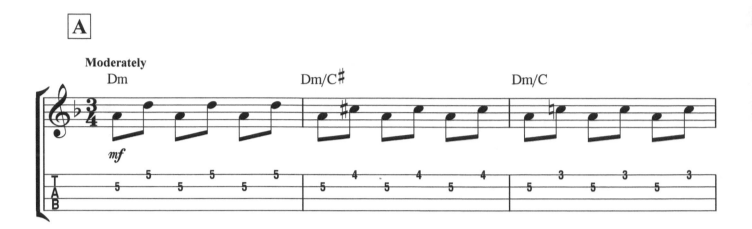

B

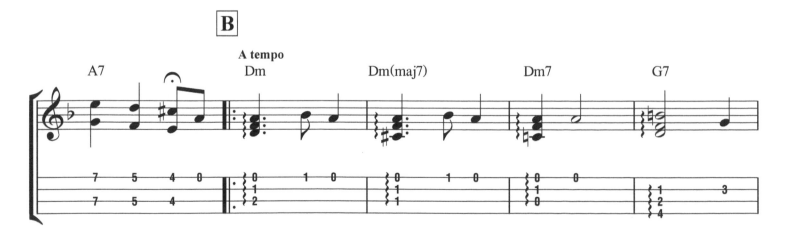

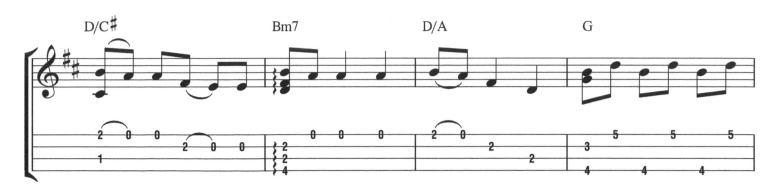

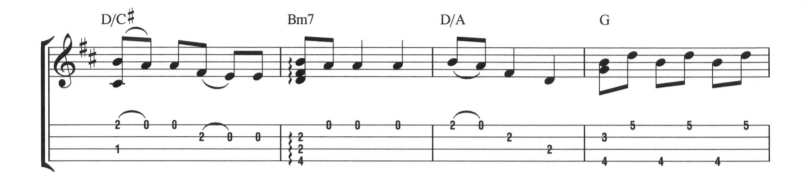

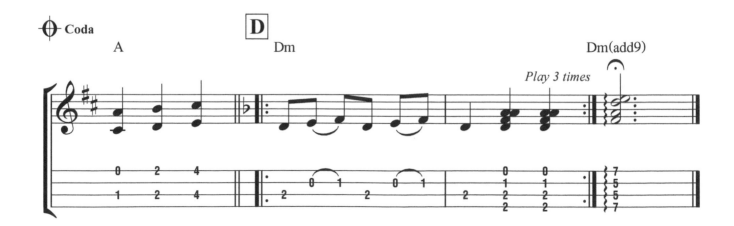

Under the Sea

from THE LITTLE MERMAID

Music by Alan Menken
Lyrics by Howard Ashman

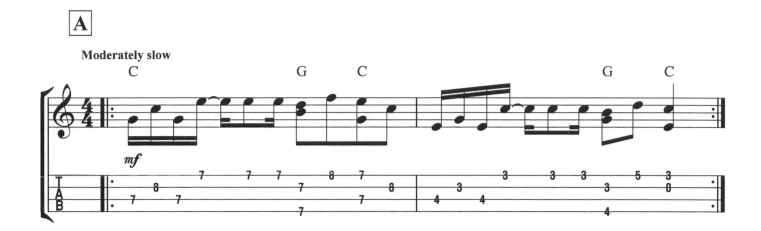

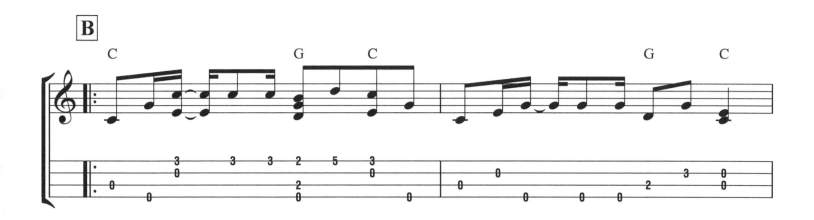

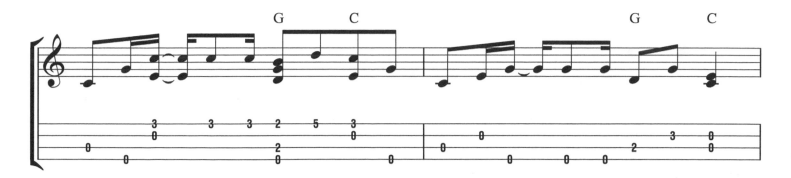

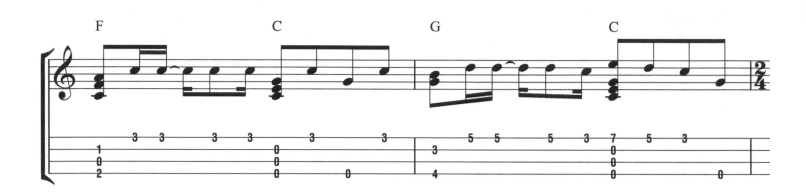

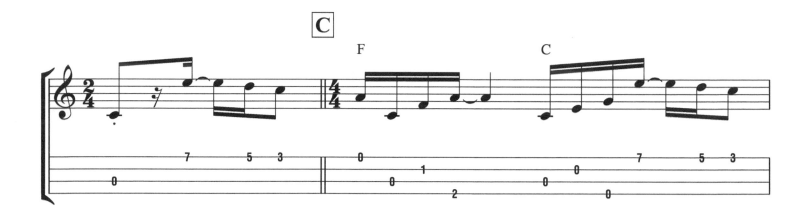

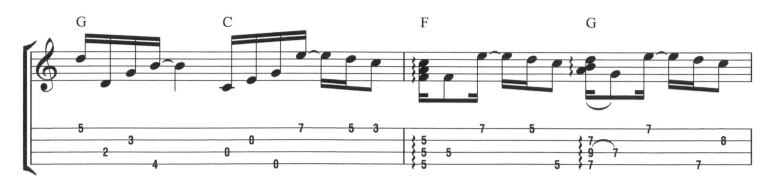

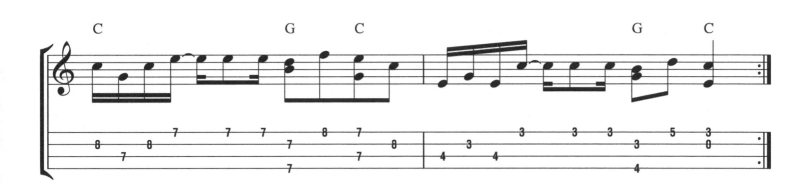

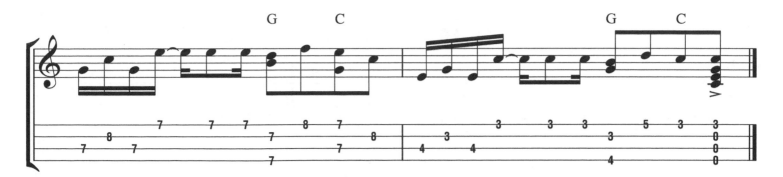

Yesterday

Words and Music by John Lennon and Paul McCartney

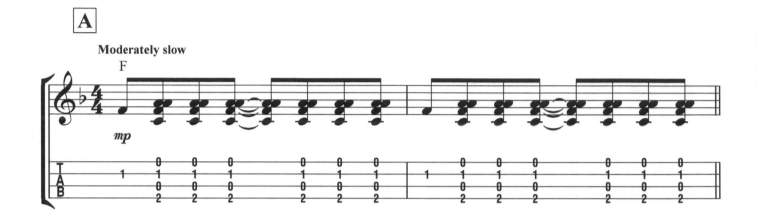

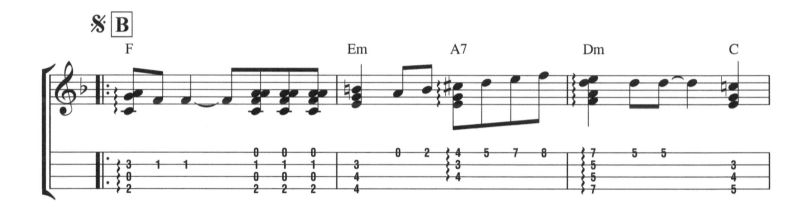

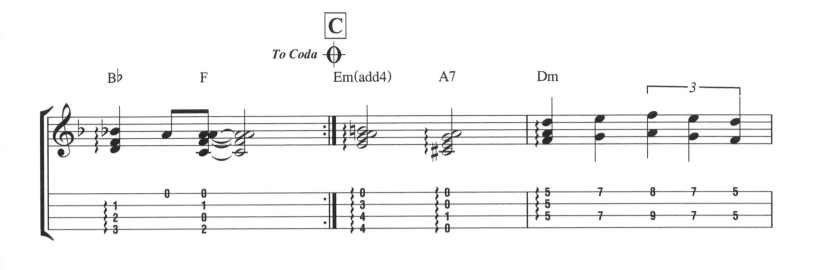

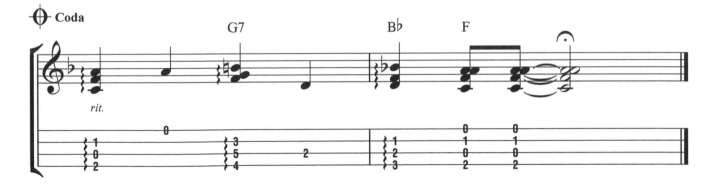

Your Song

Words and Music by Elton John and Bernie Taupin

A

B

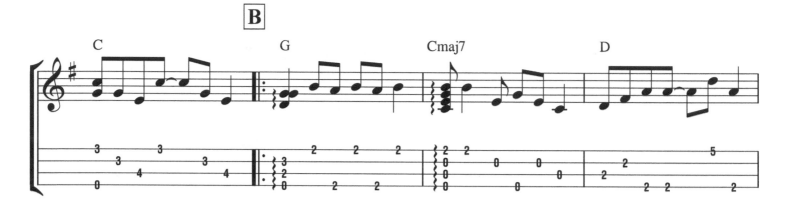

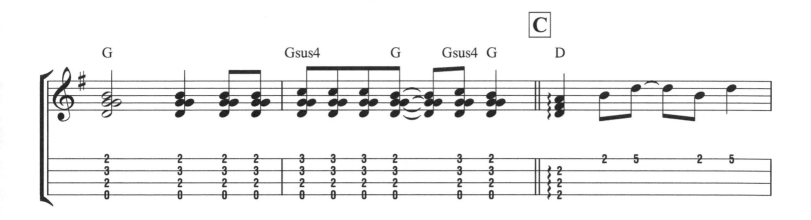

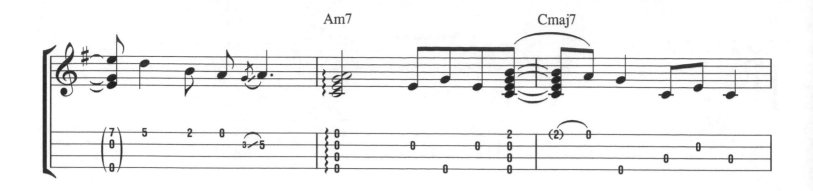

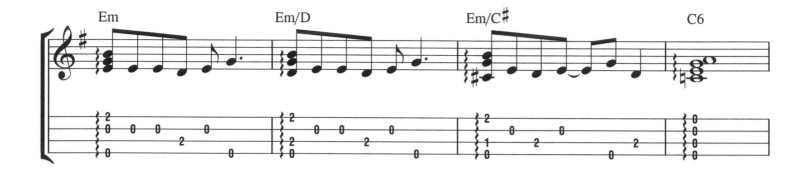

D.C. al Coda
(take repeat)

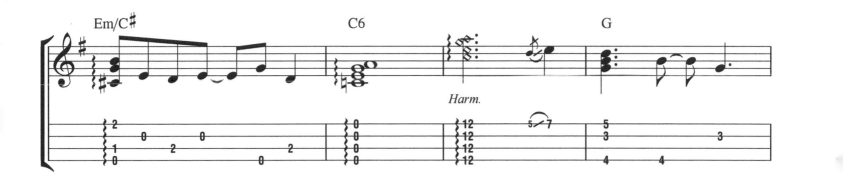

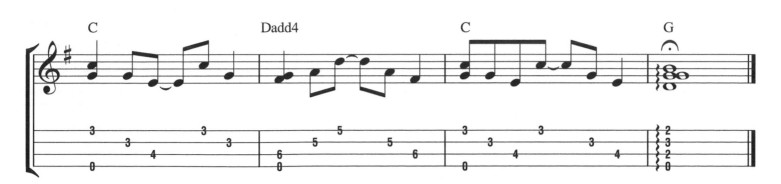

You'll Be in My Heart

from TARZAN ®
Words and Music by Phil Collins

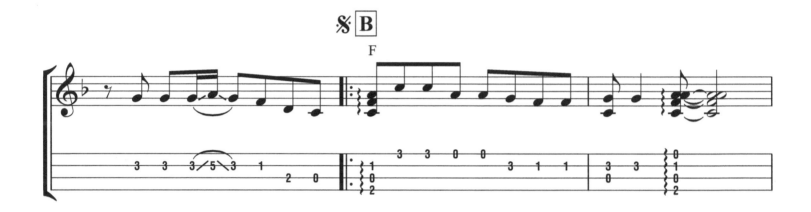

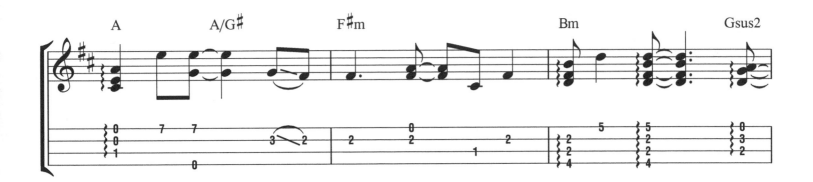

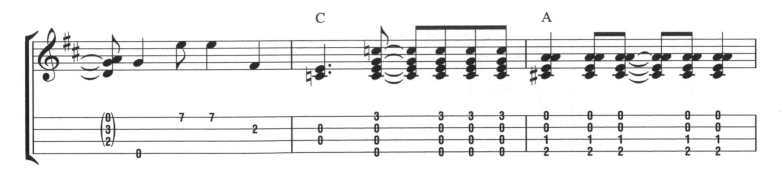

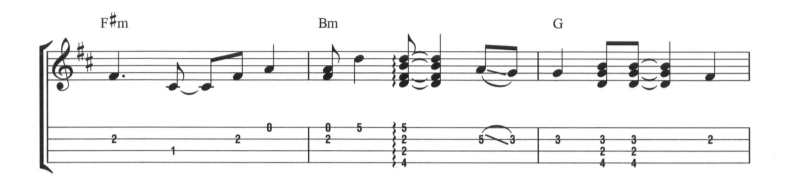